COPYRIGHT NOTICE

"It was a pleasure meeting you! Yes, I'll call your office tomorrow and we'll schedule a time when we can have lunch together! I'm looking forward to discussing all the ways we can work together."

RAVE REVIEWS FOR MYNT

"I've read books on networking. I've heard speakers try to teach networking to others. I've been to networking events where I dreaded going, because all I was ever told about networking were the basics — have a firm handshake, smile, say your name, pass out cards and have your elevator speech ready. Well? Boring! I didn't get any leads, and everyone I worked with at the event said the same thing. When I met Bart, I was blown away at how natural he was with people. Then, when I went to a networking event with him, again I was so impressed with the way he interacted with perfect strangers; how he made them feel good about themselves; how they opened right up to him within minutes of his walking in the room. I won't even mention how fast people were buying his books and asking to have their picture taken with him. Bart literally lit up the room from the moment he set foot in the door and remained the star of the night throughout the entire event. Now, THAT'S a successful networker! THAT'S how I want to enter a room, interact with others and be remembered! Don't you? The business he picked up from everyone he met was unbelievable. READ THIS BOOK and LISTEN to the AUDIO VERSION as well. You've never heard anything like it on 'networking' ... Ever!" — Mary P., Personal Coach

"You know Bart is the master at networking when his name reaches out to events he can't even attend! I was attending a women's-only award conference, when all I heard was Bart's name! 'Pat, Bart says, 'Hello'!' 'Pat, Bart says, 'Hi'!' To my total amazement, more attendees at this all-female conference seemed to know who Bart Smith was than they knew each other! Bart should have been invited to this women's-only conference just to introduce everyone to one another. He practically knew them all!" — Pat L., WomensRadio.com & AudioAcrobat.com

"Bart, as always, you are a joy to work with, ever so resourceful, a wonderful speaker and one of the best networkers I've ever met. How you go about connecting people together is amazing. When I spoke to you about setting up a networking group, I had no idea that every one who joined, both my friends and yours, all knew who you were and yet everyone there met one another for the first time. You care a lot about people and it shows. You truly are THE MARKETING MAN." — Susan L., Speaker Training

TABLE OF CONTENTS
INTRODUCTION

▶ What Is *"Networking"*?

▶ What's My Definition For *"Networking"!*

▶ What Are *"Networking Tactics"*?

▶ Who Benefits From Using *"My Networking Tactics"*?

▶ 15 Benefits From Mastering *"My Networking Tactics"!*

▶ My Top 10 *"Networking Components"!*

▶ My Secret Formula: *"Prepare, Promote, Perpetuate"*

"MY NETWORKING TACTICS"
My Top 10 "Networking Components"

"Hey, I have someone I'd like to introduce you to. Remember when you told me you needed help with (XYZ)? Well, here is just the person to help you! Allow me to introduce you to _____."

What is "Networking"?

The term "Networking," according to *Encarta's World English Dictionary* is defined as follows:

> " ... the practice of gathering of contacts: the process or practice of building up or maintaining informal relationships, especially with people whose friendship could bring advantages such as job or business opportunities."

Now, while this might satisfy a casual inquiry on the definition of this term, we need to look deeper into the meaning of "networking." In doing so, we will see that "networking" is much more than just meeting others and sharing information.

What's my definition for networking?

I believe that "networking," as it relates to business, is better defined as follows ...

> "... the progressive activity of locating, meeting and interacting with those whom we can help, who, in turn, will help us grow our business in a way that we meet both our personal and financial goals in a timely manner, and with the maximum of mutual respect with those with whom we work with, serve and assist."

Let's explore some of the logic behind my definition.

... **Who we meet** ... We need others to help grow our business. The sooner we get to them, the sooner we prosper!

... **Who we help** ... We receive by giving. The more we give, the more we get back in return and the sooner the better.

... **in turn, who will help us grow our business** ... We can't always do everything independently. We need each other!

... **meet both our personal and financial goals** ... Meeting business goals will come naturally when you excel in your business. Meeting personal goals, for most of us, is far more important in life such as spending more time with family/ friends; taking the time to be creative; playing; vacationing; sightseeing; relaxing; and more.

This requires having "financial freedom" to do the things we love to do. We all know we have to work, but let's keep our priorities straight. Working hard isn't enough. We must work smart with focus and precision! Getting help from others who may be experts in the field is the first step towards meeting your goals effectively and efficiently.

... **in a timely manner** ... This means we're not going to spend a lifetime building our businesses. We're going to work effectively so our businesses show profit within our forecasted time period -- working strategically with savvy, content-rich marketing plans!

If we follow a business model that leaves room for flexibility and expansion, the business should evolve into a success provided we met the anticipated dates of accomplishment for all sales and business activities.

... **and with the maximum of mutual respect from those with whom we work with, serve and assist.** With your hard work, integrity of the products you sell, the support and service you provide, you are well on your way to earning the respect and recognition of your clients, prospects, vendors and affiliates. You further your success by making yourself available to assist others that share your professional concerns.

By demonstrating a high degree of credibility, humility, honesty, ethical and follow-through in all your communications and business practices, people will want to work with you and buy into what you are selling.

BartSmith.com | TimeToNetwork.com | LethalConfidence.com

What are Networking Tactics?

NETWORKING TACTICS, as related to business, are really marketing-focused activities where you meet, mingle and speak with others about how you can help each other grow your businesses; expand your brands; get your names out there; find more prospects, leads, clients, customers, affiliates and vendors — to make more money and grow your business.

Who Benefits From Using "My Networking Tactics?"

People who are <u>STARTING A BUSINESS</u>! People just starting out definitely need to take advantage of networking opportunities. Why? It's low cost and virtually free to you in many ways. When you're just starting out, you'll need to:

❶ **Get the word out** about your business.

❷ **Find new leads/clients/affiliates** to help you make money.

❸ **Test/sell products and services** to others.

❹ **Find/hire vendors and/or specialty consultants** to help your business. There will be more on these topics later.

People who are <u>GROWING A BUSINESS</u>! No matter what stage your business is at, you'll always need to:

❶ **Continue to promote yourself** and your business.

❷ **Find new leads/clients/affiliates/suppliers.**

❸ **Test/sell products and services** to others.

For business owners on a **<u>MARKETING BUDGET</u>**, some of your biggest clients can be the result of attending just one meeting. <u>More than 60 percent of all consulting contracts</u> come from networking versus cold calls, bulk mailings or other approaches that require "interruption marketing tactics" that are not recommended and don't work!

15 Benefits For Mastering "My" Networking Tactics!

There are at least 15 important reasons why you need to master the art of **networking** and **networking tactics** outlined in this book to be successful:

(1) Find new leads, clients and customers to make money.

(2) Sell product/services on the spot to make money.

(3) Find others to help you develop new products/services such as joint venture partners.

(4) Find people who can help sell your products/services such as affiliates.

(5) Get more exposure for you and your business using both free and low cost marketing tactics, such as ... *networking!*

(6) Save time and money using resources more effectively. Achieve greater results in less time by meeting several prospects in one place.

(7) Cautiously test the market with new, innovative products/ services/ideas for financial growth.

(8) Find new vendors/service providers to help grow your business such as specialty consultants, merchants and material suppliers.

(9) Practice your "pitch" and your "story-telling" techniques.

(10) Share advice, ideas and resources with others to share your expertise and willingness to support their ventures.

(11) Be seen and heard at events to build recognition and credibility.

(12) Share residual/commission-based products/services with others and make even more money with passive income received on a regular basis with little effort required to maintain it.

(13) Remain current with the times. Learn what's new. Stay a few steps ahead of the game so you know what's happening in your industry and how it impacts others.

(14) Socialize. Get out of your home office and meet new people in your line of business such as attending a presentation by a noted speaker. Working in a vacuum never gets results!

(15) Stimulate continued growth for your business! Keep building your list so you have a never-ending flow of solid leads, prospects, clients, affiliates and vendors to grow your business.

These Are My TOP 10 "Networking Components!"

When it comes to networking like a *skilled* professional, there are ten key components to understand and master if you want to get the most out of networking with others.

#1 TARGET MARKET: WHO is your target? Who do you need to reach out to for assistance or advice to grow your business, buy your products or services, conduct seminars, or acquire speaking engagements? Do you need vendors and/or service providers, customers/clients or joint venture partners to grow and expand your business? Know where your business is at, what your business' needs are and where to locate these targeted people. Where do **they** mingle, mix and socialize because you want to be there?

#2 LOCATIONS: WHERE can you find people to network with? Make a list of places, events, workshops, associations, clubs, organizations, groups and their locations and when they meet. How much will it cost to access any of these groups? Each will present different opportunities to help you accomplish your networking goals.

#3 GOALS: Know your GOALS for each networking event. For every event you attend, you should know ahead of time what your objectives are. What do you hope to gain? Know your goals and document them. You may have different goals for each networking event you attend.

#4 TOOLS: How will you ORGANIZE your networking activities? You'll need all the right networking TOOLS already in place to keep your networking efforts well organized. This effort will pay off.

#5 RESOURCES: In order to be an effective networker, you will need a number of resources that you can refer to as well as share with others -- all with the same goal of how to make money, alliances and more.

#6 PREPARATIONS: Research, rehearse and practice! Research the company, their staff and those that supply services to them. Rehearse every detail of your presentation with examples of what you can bring to the table right down to what you'll wear. PREPARE to network!

#7 PRESENCE: How you LOOK, walk, stand, talk, hold your hands and position your shoulders (body language) can speak volumes about you. First impressions make all the difference when networking and you only get ONE chance. What they say about you after you're gone means more to your success than what they say directly to you. Your success depends on selling YOU!

#8 CONVERSATIONS: What you SAY, how you say it, the questions; you ask, questions you *don't* ask, knowing when to speak up and when *not* to will assuredly affect your success at networking.

#9 ACTIONS: What you DO BEFORE, DURING and AFTER the networking event are very important and will be noted by others. Importantly, know the rules of etiquette, manners, gestures and mannerisms to help you skate through the networking process. This is especially important when dealing with other business cultures.

#10 FUTURE GROWTH: Once the networking event has ended, how will you NURTURE the contacts you made? You must maintain steady and effective communication to further your business needs? My follow-up techniques teach you how to keep the "light on" with business relationships, which is vital to your success.

Learn To Network Like A Pro

Networking effectively (like many marketing tactics) is a *learned skill!* All you need is someone to coach you on the steps.

Effective networking is not about "selling" or "shameless promotion." It's about asking people (1) what they do, (2) listening to ways you might be able to help them and from that (one-sided) conversation, (3) determining if this person can help you with your business needs. Are they a potential client? Would you feel comfortable working with them?

You'll learn by **listening** more and asking the right questions. Are they a potential vendor/service provider? Can you check the person or their company on the Internet? Can this person refer leads to you? Will the referrals need to be prescreened or qualified? Can you access the people that have the knowledge you need?

What else can you learn from talking to people you meet? ASK, LISTEN and you will LEARN!

> **"We are warmed by fire, not by the smoke of the fire. We are carried over the sea by a ship, not by the wake of a ship. So too, what we are is to be sought in the invisible depths of our own being, not in our outward reflection in our own acts. We must find our real selves not in the froth stirred up by the impact of our being upon the beings around us, but in our own soul which is the principle of all our acts."**
>
> – *No Man Is An Island, Thomas Merton*

My Secret Formula:
(The 3 Ps for Networking)
Prepare ▶ Promote ▶ Perpetuate

Our everyday work ambition should be to enjoy what we do, to increase profitability and to have the freedom to put into practice what we learn. To do that, we need to use every networking opportunity available to us to create and strengthen those contacts, to choose the right networking style, and learn how to read people.

The networking world is a diverse one, so use it to your advantage. Don't hesitate to capitalize on gender, senior groups, minorities, and others if there is evidence that these groups can use your products or services. In fact, finding a **mentor** who can direct your networking efforts is the ultimate networking contact.

Networking is for all levels of business savvy. If you are just starting out (for example) and do not expect to be a source of critical, rich business expertise necessary for all business types and sizes to depend on, this information is for you.

The psychology of asking for help in any arena can be difficult for some people. Most, however, appreciate being asked for help and feel like champions when they can be of some value. Doesn't everyone like to be considered an expert? Generally, the pros are motivated to help the newcomer.

The best business networking groups operate as exchanges of business information, ideas, and support. It is not enough to attend a networking function, meet lots of people, collect all of their business cards, and then go home and try to sort it all out. This is not a plan and you need to have a *real* plan! Master networkers have been enormously successful using this theory: *Gain by giving! Gain by giving is the foundation for networking.*

Once you become a convincing networking expert, you may wish to start your own networking club. Think of the possibilities!

BartSmith.com | TimeToNetwork.com | LethalConfidence.com

Helping others connect, you quickly become the go-to resource in your field.

Remember, networking is not about how many hands you shake. It is more about who you know! The expert networker makes a commitment to learn everything he/she needs to know about the business and practices a number of tactics to effectively reach out to people by creating value.

Genuinely,

Bart Smith

BARTSMITH.COM

TheMarketingMan.com

TimeToNetwork.com

BartSmith.com

RichCoachBrokeCoach.com

CoachingClientForms.com

FindTheOneForMe.com

SpeakerCafe.com

TVGuest.com

BreakThroughBS.com

iLoveBartsCookies.com

BartsCookies.com

... and many more!

WARNING: You are about to learn my "personal secrets" to networking like a master networking professional with an accelerated level of confidence and marketing precision. Use these networking tools, tactics, techniques and tricks at your own risk! They should lead you to an increase in your income and a few new friendships!

NETWORKING COMPONENT #1

TARGET MARKET

Survey your business needs!
Where do you need help?

Do you need help finding new clients or making sales? Do you need help balancing the books? BEFORE you start talking to people, fully understand your business needs.

Make a detailed list of your needs. Then, assign an occupation (an expert in your field that can assist you). For example:

❑ Need <u>to form a business</u>? Find a <u>business structure specialist</u>.

❑ Need help <u>saving money on your taxes</u>? Find a *good* <u>accountant</u>.

❑ Need <u>clients</u>? Find <u>others</u> who <u>compliment</u> your <u>occupation</u>.

❑ Need a <u>website</u>? Find a <u>webmaster</u> to build one for you.

❑ Need a <u>shopping cart</u>? Find an <u>Internet marketing specialist</u>.

❑ Need <u>affiliates</u>? Find people who want to make money!

❑ Need help <u>making sales</u>? Find <u>affiliates</u> to help sell for you.

❑ Need help <u>expanding your brand</u>? Find a <u>marketing specialist</u>.

❑ Need to <u>get hired to speak</u>? Find <u>people</u> who run events.

❑ Need to get <u>on the radio/TV</u>? Find a <u>radio/TV publicity expert</u>.

❑ Need <u>investment money</u>? Find <u>people who invest</u> in businesses.

Knowing WHO you need to contact BEFORE you begin researching can save you valuable time. It's all about doing your homework!

Don't hesitate to list ALL of your business needs no matter how insignificant. This is not a waste of your time.

Remember, for every need your business does not address in a timely manner, you may be losing time and money because you are not operating at absolute efficiency!

Make another list of the kind of people you would like to meet who might be able to help you with your business!

Similar to the list you made in Tactic #1, this list refers to the "kinds" of people you'd like to meet that can help you with your business. This list could include potential JV partners, specific vendors, customers, clients, affiliates, material suppliers, merchants, meeting/event planners, seminar facilitators, etc.

These are people about whom you suspect "something good" might come from the two of you meeting. The sooner you meet, the better for the both of you! So, make a list of these kinds of people! More specific, these people might include:

PEOPLE YOU KNOW, BUT HAVE NEVER MET IN PERSON

Schedule a time when the two of you can get together. Drive to their place of business or meet half way! But MEET! If you're traveling into their area for business, schedule a meeting with them before/after your other intended meeting. When I lived in Orange County, California, and traveled to Los Angeles, California, I always called on a few associates in the business to see if they would be interested in my stopping by their place of business/ residence. And guess what? They all said, "Yes!" Well, that is if they were available! You see, people love socializing with whom they do business! Especially, when they don't get to see you that often!

What if they live out of state? Are they going to be visiting near where you live any time soon? Would you be willing to drive a little distance to meet them? When I heard that a client of mine from Arizona was visiting a Southern California theme park with his family, I drove almost two hours just to visit with him for an hour. Was it worth it? YES! Our business relationship is that much stronger today for it! He was very appreciative of my coming down and I appreciated that his family permitted me some quality time with my client. Go out of your way to meet folks face to face whenever you can. You may never get the chance again.

PEOPLE YOU KNOW, BUT HAVEN'T HEARD FROM IN A LONG TIME

Out of sight -- out of mind! One way to rekindle dormant business relationships is to call the individual. Email and text messages are okay, but make a personal phone call first. There's nothing wrong with social media, but you can't shake someone's hand even virtually. Online has to become offline at some point. Consider inviting your contact to breakfast, lunch or dinner to discuss what's new and exciting to bring him/her back into the loop.

PEOPLE YOU HAVEN'T MET, YET!

By now, you have a good list of professionals that were highly recommend to you and you've been following them through their newsletters and blogs. Now, set time aside to contact them. Mention something unique and positive about their product/ service to open the door to having more close-range conversations on how you can help each other. If you need to ask for a favor such as a referral, do so. You know the feeling when someone asks you for help. You're flattered to oblige. Most people are.

> **"I've always wanted to meet you! I get your online eZine. It's just filled with useful tips. I was wondering ..."**
>
> **"I always learn something from your website, product, e-Course, presentation, audio recording, etc."**
>
> **"I bought your (book/product) and have a question ..."**
>
> **"(Name) referred me to you and suggested we meet to discuss how we might work together."**
>
> **"Can you tell me more about your product offers?"**

Once these people get to know you and you get to know them, assess any opportunities that might come from meeting them such as JVs, affiliate relationships, speaking engagements, referrals and so much more.

It's not always who YOU know, but who OTHER PEOPLE KNOW that can help you get what you want in life and in business!

You never know when that one person you dismissed as a prospect for your business could lead you to someone who actually could! The lesson here is a simple one. Don't turn anyone away! Treat every contact you make with respect and sincerity because you never know where it will lead. That's the Golden Rule: Treat others how you would like to be treated.

Being a professional means you demonstrate what you know without being a know-it-all. When you meet someone new you should be thinking about what you can do to help that person, not what he or she can do to help you. Your attitude towards others can motivate them to introduce you to potentially viable clients that can grow your business and marketing plans. You're in business to make a profit. Don't turn potential money away.

Let's redefine the word "Stranger" to become something more appealing and more effective for accomplishing our networking goals!

When we were children, we were told not to talk to strangers. That was for our protection. In business today, it is VITAL that we do talk to strangers! They have become the lifeblood for every thriving business. We can't keep selling to our friends and family. We have to reach out to unknowns we haven't met yet!

So, to diffuse the stigma about talking to strangers, let's turn it into something more effective. Make a good first impression when meeting new people. They will think you are a brilliant conversationalist as you listen to 2/3 of the conversation. These strangers are about to become your best friends, advocates, customers, resources, etc. Remember, you are a stranger to them as well so ask a few easy questions and get them talking about their needs, wants, desires, ideas, answers, resources, marketing/partnership opportunities for starters. Share your passions and special interests to give others some idea of what's important to you and how they can relate.

Before attending your next networking event, think of the audience you're about to engage with and remember that there are no strangers in business:

> **I no longer think of people as strangers. We all share similar needs in business and in life. Everyone in this room has a common goal, and that is to meet someone who can help you with your business. I am one of those people. So, all we have to do is listen, enjoy the camaraderie and share what we know or have learned. Invite others to join the conversation. Work together to achieve mutual goals. That's how networking works! Allow me to introduce myself, my name is _____.**

Ask your friends and associates in the business, "Who do you know who can help me with _____?"

When in doubt, ASK friends and associates by networking within your immediate circle of contacts. These referrals are a great way to ease your way into meeting new people that can assist you. Here are a couple of sample questions to get started:

Who did you use to design your ____?
(i.e., website, postcards, brochure, flyers, book, ...)

How did you like his/her work?
(i.e., are they any good, would you recommend them, ...)

Would you mind if I called them?
(i.e., ask permission as these are not your contacts, yet, ...)

When you call on a referral, you might try initiating the conversation with the following ...

> **"Hi, (your friend's name), referred me to you."**
> (Identify WHO referred you.)
>
> **"They said you might be able to help me with _____?"**
> (Identify WHY they referred you.)
>
> **Are you available to speak right now?**
> (Be courteous, and always ask if it is a good time to speak.)

Once, you've got the "green light" to speak, be as clear as possible in your request for help. Respect their time, and always say:

"Thank you, for your time. I really appreciate your help."

Courtesy and excellent phone etiquette go a long way in making new friends in the business. Who knows when a referral can bring you more business than you can handle! Treasure every contact you make.

Network to find the following key people you need to know!

When emergencies strike and you need help, here are the people you need to know on a first-name basis. Treat them like gold, send them greeting cards, take them to lunch, visit with them periodically or call them.

1. Accountants/Tax Preparers
2. Computer Repair Experts
3. Dentist/Doctors
4. Graphic Designers
5. Hair Stylists
6. Investors/Fundraisers
7. Lawyers/Attorneys
8. Locksmiths
9. Mechanics
10. Publicists
11. Vendors/Suppliers
12. Video/Audio Experts
13. Virtual Assistants
14. Webmasters

You may want to expand your list for services that only a plumber, notary, bank manager, etc. can provide. Don't be caught unprepared in business or in your personal life without ready resources!

NETWORKING COMPONENT #2

LOCATION

*Hello, I was wondering when your group usually meets? I'd like to attend one of your events. May I have directions to your location ... and, your name is _____?
Thank you. I'll plan to see you there.
Yes, I'll bring plenty of business cards!"*

Once you know WHO you need to contact, find out WHERE they meet and GET THERE quick!

From the list of people you need to meet, now make a list of all the places you think you might find them.

> Meetups, Seminars, Classes, Workshops, Coffee Shops, Networking Events, Associations, Conferences, Chamber Of Commerce, Social Clubs, Hobby Clubs, Round Tables, Focus Groups, Mastermind Groups, Charity Events, Religious Events, Conventions, Expos, Trade Shows, etc.

Within each of these categories, there are potentially thousands of people waiting to meet you. Locate the companies and business networking organizations that run events in your vicinity that support your topics of interest.

Schedule time to call these organizations to find out what they do, how they operate and when they meet. Plan to attend one of their meetings or events. Think of the potential leads!

> **"Hi, can you tell me about your company?"**
>
> **"Yes, hi, I was wondering when your group meets?"**
>
> **"Is there a fee to attend your group/class/meeting?"**
>
> **"Do you have a website?"**
>
> **"Great, can I bring a friend?"**
>
> **"Great, I look forward to meeting you ..."**
>
> **"I'll ask for you when I get there ..."**
>
> **"See you then ..."**

In the upcoming sections of this book, I will cover what to take to these events, how to prepare, what to say, how to organize and how to make the most of your networking efforts with others.

Network With Others Online

You don't need to leave your house or office to network with other people. You can use the Internet to meet hundreds, even thousands of other people that can help you find solutions to your business' needs. In order to network on the Internet, check out these locations, what to do when you get there and how often:

WHERE = BLOGS, VIDEO SHARING WEBSITES, REVIEW WEBSITES, ONLINE FORUMS, COMMENT/FEEDBACK AREAS, MESSAGE BOARDS, DISCUSSION BOARDS, etc.) ... What topic, products, services, or _____ interest you? Find them online and no doubt those websites usually have a forum or some form of message board for you to provide comments and feedback for their members to benefit from. Find your passion online and strike up a conversation, discussion, debate or anything else related to communicating with others. What a fast way to network and meet new people who share your common interests.

HOW[1] = PROVIDE FEEDBACK, ANSWER QUESTIONS! You can collaborate, offer ideas to explore new topics, discuss the issues, ask questions and answer them as well. Quora.com is a great example where you can create a profile (showcasing your expertise) and provide answers to questions from every day folks. Questions range from personal interest all the way to business.

HOW[2] = MOBILE APPS ... Who says you can't look up networking events and network with others using your phone? This is the age right? Try these apps on for size: Shapr (Android and iOS), Bizzabo (Android and iOS), CityHour (iOS), 1 Million Cups (Android, iOS, and Web), FullContact (Android, iOS, and Web) and Clearbit Connect (Gmail, Web). You might also look into PROsimity.com, ContentPlum.com, TagBoard.com, and Whova.com.

HOW[3] = WEBSITE CONTACT FORM & COLD EMAILING ... If you're anxious to get the conversation going with someone, contact them through their website contact form or send them an eMail. I've done that successfully and people have done the same to me.

WHEN = OFTEN! ... Become a regular at any of these websites to become a trusted figure who people look to for great advice.

Network Using Social Media!

Get ready to meet hundreds, if not thousands, of people online via social media. Here are some of the more popular websites where you can meet, greet, and grow your social network ... ONLINE!

- **Meetup.com**: If you're familiar with this website it's a huge online social networking portal that facilitates offline group meetings in cities around the world. This is by far the first and easiest way to start networking offline. What's your passion, interest or hobby? If you can't find it on Meetup.com, start your own MeetUp group and start your own networking with like-minded people.

- **Facebook.com** — Who isn't on Facebook? The best part about using Facebook.com to network with others online, besides the actual networking, are all the great features, bells and whistles Facebook offers to HELP you network with others. For example, join and/or start your own Facebook Group, build a Fan Page to promote your brand and attract customers, run ads to reach your target market, etc. You can find me at **Facebook.com/bartscookies**.

- **LinkedIn.com** — With LinkedIn, you can find the people, jobs, groups, advice and services you need through people you come to know and trust while strengthening and extending your existing network. Many of the people you need to reach already use LinkedIn. So, why not search for them now? Do you have a LinkedIn profile? If you don't, build one. If you do, is it complete? This is the #1 networking website for showcasing your professional side. While the other networking sites tend to be more "social" in nature, LinkedIn is for professionals like you and I. With millions of members, I'm sure you can find the contacts you need at every level and in thousands of industries. Set up your LinkedIn.com account today and connect with me at **LinkedIn.com/in/bartsmith**.

- **Twitter.com** — Do you "tweet?" If so, great! If not, isn't it time you started? Join the conversation with thousands of topics and other folks on Twitter. People can follow you and get to know who you are and what you do. Tweet (post) what you're up to daily on Twitter. You can post pictures, links, news announcements, advice, resources, videos, and more. You can find me at **Twitter.com/ bartsmith**.

- **Bebo.com**: In the UK, Bebo is a huge social network. Bebo allows users to create social networking profiles for free, and offers them many of the same features as other social networking websites. You can upload photos, videos and all kinds of other information. The site boasts users from more than a dozen countries, including the USA, Australia, Canada, France, Poland, and Germany.

- **Ning.com**: Ning takes social networking to a new level. They allow you to create your own social network community with your own custom domain name in addition to offering you a bevvy of tools, features, bells and whistles to help enhance your users' experience in meeting other people in your community. Some of the biggest organizers, activists and influencers in the world use Ning to create online social experiences that help inspire action. Thinking about starting your own online social group? Check out Ning. com and all they have to offer.

Online Search For Networking Events

Go online and search for networking events in your local area or neighboring counties, nationwide or even worldwide. You can also find many networking groups online by going to Google.com or using your favorite search engine. Enter any combination of the following key words for searches:

- Your <u>Expertise</u> + **Key Word** *(See Next Page)*
- Your <u>Town, State</u> + **Key Word** *(See Next Page)*
- Your <u>Industry</u> + **Key Word** *(See Next Page)*
- Your <u>Hobby</u> + **Key Word** *(See Next Page)*
- Your <u>Interest</u> + **Key Word** *(See Next Page)*

Then, search by the *"key words"* below and you're bound to find something in your local area, within driving distance, regionally, nationally and worldwide.

"business conventions"	**"national expos"**
"business expos"	**"national meetings"**
"business hangouts"	**"national tradeshows"**
"business meetings"	**"networking events"**
"business mixers"	**"networking mixers"**
"business networking"	**"social hangouts"**
"business tradeshows"	**"social meetings"**
"national conventions"	**"social mixers"**

To Pay or Not to Pay

That is the question! If you're just starting out, go to all of the FREE networking events you can. By doing so, you acquire plenty of opportunity to test your skills, practice your story-telling techniques at no cost with the exception of a little time, maybe and gas money. Exhaust all the free events in your area for leads, ideas, and referrals before you consider paying to attend an event.

If there are ten free events scheduled every month in your area, attend at least a few of them. Don't worry about attending the events that charge a fee until you've capitalized on all the free ones unless you know your friends are going to be at a particular event that costs money to enter.

Make it a point to exhaust all the free opportunities to network and socialize, including Internet websites, before attending events that cost money or even websites that might charge for special account privileges or extra services.

Return On Investment (ROI)

When it comes to attending events that will cost money, there's one rule to keep in mind:

Return **O**n **I**nvestment

If you invest $30 at the door to attend a networking event, are you going to be able to walk away (1-2 hours later) with leads, ideas for a new product/service, sales (at the event) or in the near future?

Maybe you attended an event, which required you to pay at the door, and you found one person who turned out to be a big affiliate for you! Let's say the affiliate had 15,000 subscribers on their eZine list who would be very interested in what you have to sell/offer. Perhaps, from that one contact, you secured a speaking engagement that paid $2,500. The potential to gain financially from either of these contacts was worth the price of attending an event that charged #30. You don't always have to walk away with a huge gain or tons of leads. There's value in *every* meeting. Just be patient and look for it!

When you are not getting a return on your investment (time, money/cost to attend) at networking events that cost you money ... STOP GOING! Consider purchasing an annual membership at some of these networking organizations that offer them. Some have non-member fees and member-only door fees. Sometimes, fees are waived for newcomers. Ask. Then, make it a point to talk to every member possible. You certainly don't want to be networking with a group of people who don't grow, don't change or bring in any new members, right? Here are a few sample questions to ask:

> **"How long have you been a member of (organization)?"**
>
> **"What has your membership done for your business?"**
>
> **"How many members does the organization add each year ... every six months?**
>
> **Has the organization continued to grow?"**

Networking is great for sharing your knowledge and communicating on common interests. It's a good way to get feedback on new ideas and ask for suggestions on pitfalls and problems. In these get-togethers, you are talking to a choir that speaks your language.

Now, if you think you're not getting something tangible or of value such as a lead, sale, business card, new names, ideas, etc., don't think you're wasting your time (or money).

At a minimum – TAKE YOUR CELL PHONE or CAMERA to the event and TAKE PICTURES of yourself with other people at the event, the event host, meeting planner or speaker at the event. Sometimes people will put these key photos on a website ... just make sure you get the permission of the individual you photograph.

Link to the event or the website hosting from the *Press Room* on your website. Document your activities whenever you socialize with other business people. Your clients and customers will see that you're active and a people person. When they see you smiling and socializing with others, they instinctively develop confidence and trust in you. Success breeds more success and people will want what you have to offer.

Don't think you have to walk away with something tangible. **Intangible** benefits can last a lifetime. When people see your photos in your website's *Press Room*, it serves as a testament to the fact that you are approachable, professional, and someone they might like to do business with. Any good impression can create activity for your business.

To recap, exhaust all the FREE opportunities to socialize and network before considering events that cost money. Investigate the membership benefits for these organizations. Can they give you the kind of marketing, exposure and publicity you need to promote and grow your enterprise offline, even online? Staying visible and being recognized is a big benefit of networking. This can you help to build your reputation that can only generate more leads and referrals and more business.

Look online in your local newspapers, magazines and community publications for mixers and other networking events!

Finding new prospects can be as close as your doorstep. Just look in the *Business Section, Local Events/Meetings, Lifestyle, Entertainment* or similar section of your local newspaper.

Typically, these events are located in the same section of the paper each week. Make a few phone calls and talk to the coordinators of these events. Tell them a little about yourself. They'll be enthused to learn that a new person is planning to attend their event.

Then, when you arrive at the event, you already have a contact from your phone conversation. Be sure you locate that person that may prove invaluable to you. Introduce yourself to as many people as you can. Get their cards or contact information. That's what networking is all about — people meeting people in all kinds of places, both online and off.

Remember, it's not just a one-way street. If a person you meet is in your network and he/she matches a business you encounter at one of your events, then share the details. It can only strengthen your relationships and it gives a great impression to others about how you operate.

NETWORKING COMPONENT #3

GOALS

What Are Your Goals For Networking?

What are your GOALS for each networking event you attend?

Here are some suggestions on a set of goals you might want to accomplish at your next event:

- **Why are you going?** ... to find new leads, new vendors, new affiliates, etc.

- **Who do you want to meet?** ... key contacts, the meeting attendees, speaker(s), the meeting planner, potential customers, etc.

- **What do you want to share with those you meet?** ... your products/services, affiliate program, new idea, press releases, resources, audio programs, etc.)

- **What do you hope to walk away with?** ... new leads, business cards, new vendor resources, sales, photographs, future meetings/appointments, etc.)

It might be helpful to review *Networking Component #1: TARGET MARKET – Who* do you need to meet that can help you with your business? Analyze your business needs? What do you need to help grow your business? It will be these kinds of people who you will need to look for and meet, specifically! Be well-informed about your business situation so you can articulate clearly and briefly what your needs are. You want to be able to make your point and make an impression.

Knowing your BUSINESS' NEEDS will help you to identify your goals and zero in on what you need to gain from that meeting!

- **Know WHO** you need to contact before you go looking for them will save you time.

- **Know WHERE** to look for these people will save you time and money.

- **Know WHAT** your goals are will guarantee that you are on the right track for mastering success in your business.

Know exactly what you want to get out of the networking event. By surrounding yourself with people who share your drive and ambition, you are more likely to move ahead with even more clarity and be inspired to do your best work.

Expect The Unexpected And Respond Accordingly!

You never know who will be at a networking. Be on the lookout for special opportunities to meet certain people, participate in activities, go with certain groups, and offer unique ideas, solutions and resources.

If you're not sure that the people you find at a networking event can help you, don't feel obligated to stay unless you think these people can turn you on to others who are not in attendance. Otherwise, save you time for preparing for the next networking event. Remember, time is money, especially when you're networking.

Build A Network Of People You Know, Not Just For Your Own Benefit, But For The Benefit Of Others You Know.

One of your networking goals should always be to build a network of people that you can share! Very few people actually walk away from a networking event with a contract ... because at the heart of networking, what you really want is contacts and lots of them.

The first step for networking is to meet people, then it's what you do afterwards that really counts. Develop your leads, and, if you aren't finding what you need, you may know someone who does. Watch your list grow, along with your reputation, whether it's for fun or business. In the long run, you are always a winner because you got out there and networked.

Find ways to put new people together and make introductions at every turn. When you make a new acquaintance, introduce them to all of your contacts, or at least the ones you believe they might need to meet first.

Example: "Gayl, have you met my friend Dr. Purcell? She's a naturopathic doctor looking for interview and media training. I believe that she too could benefit from one of your radio tours. You might discover some interesting business opportunities as you get to know each other."

Example: "John, you should speak with Anne. She's the account representative for the company that printed my books. Maybe she can give you a competitive rate on printing your new book. Here's her telephone number. Tell her I referred you and she'll treat you like family."

Example: "Peter, please say hello to my friend Lola. She needs to get a merchant account so she can accept payments from her coaching clients. Please set her up with everything she needs. Lola, say hello to Peter ..."

When you grow other people's businesses, guess who they'll think of when they need to refer someone in need of your services. That's right ... YOU!

Turn Every Interaction With Human Beings Into A Networking Event!

With every networking event you attend, with every new introduction you make, with every interaction ... no matter where you go (party, restaurant, local bar/cafe, airport, waiting in line at the grocery store, etc.), make it your goal to turn every interaction into a *"How can I help you?"* networking event! Spin every meeting into an opportunity to find new leads for your products and services and for others. Secure new affiliates to help sell your products. Find speaking gigs, new vendors, and material suppliers, and future product/joint venture partners, etc. Typically, three to five new leads is perfect! Want more? Then, all you have to do is network more!

My Personal Goals For Attending Networking Events

Depending on the type of networking event whether it's for five people or 105, in order to become connected to key influencers in my industry and within my target market, having done some research on the event, this is what I aim to accomplish:

NETWORKING GOAL #1: PHOTOGRAPHS

ALWAYS TAKE YOUR CELL PHONE OR A DIGITAL CAMERA TO AN EVENT. As soon as you arrive at the event, greet the person who invited you to the event and ask to have a picture taken with you. It's my way of saying, *"Thank you for inviting me to this event. I want to capture this networking moment with you. Smile!"*

Your contact will also appreciate you when the flash of your camera sends a shock wave of interest in your direction. People will be curious and inquire, *"Who just took a picture and who's in it?"*

You can imagine people saying, *"Hey, who's that guy/gal having their picture taken with (so and so)? Should I meet them? Yes, I will!"* Their interest will peak when you make a celebrity-style entrance! Consider taking a picture with (almost) everyone you meet. You don't have to use them all, but you'll have them just in case.

Take pictures of banners, stage props, posters and the restaurant or hotel sign where the event is taking place especially if it's a particularly grand hotel or a restaurant. Take a picture of the owner. Even the servants who are servicing the event no doubt wouldn't mind participating in a little fun. You're just spreading the joy and bringing attention to some hard workers. And, guess who's going to see you do all this? That's right, the event host or meeting planner!

This is a good way to stand out in a crowd in a positive way that doesn't annoy guests and participants. You'll get even more interest and leads that way. More people will want to work with you, which is your goal, right?

Naturally, take pictures with the speakers, the meeting planner or event coordinator. Offer to take other people's pictures and offer to eMail the picture to them. Oh, get their business card!

What a great ice-breaker! *"Hey, if you give me your card, I'll send you the photo ... and, I just know we'll be doing some business together ..."* It's a great way to be remembered and to remember them. You have their photo!

Practice getting your picture taken a lot. If you have a camera on a cell phone, practice at home with someone. SMILE! SMILE! SMILE! WORK ON THAT SMILE! Know what to wear that makes you look good. How do you like your hair? Are you in good shape? Work out. Take care of *you* so your photos represent your best side.

However, don't let size, height or shape get in your way of a photograph. The #1 factor that makes every photograph a winner is not fancy clothing or a perfect haircut. It's that winning smile that communicates confidence, congeniality, and optimism.

What Should You Do With All The Pictures You Take?

Post them on your website, in your online newsletter (or eZine), in your blog, across all of your social media accounts, in your online press room, press kit, *About Us* page, *Events* page if you have one, home page, etc. Get ideas from other people and post your pictures as they do and *where* they do if possible. Just imagine the number of new visitors to your website that will see you photographed working a networking event? Be seen. Get hired!

NETWORKING GOAL #2: INTRODUCTIONS

You **want** to meet speakers, meeting planners, contacts and friends, everywhere! When I meet them, I'm not interested in telling them my story up front. There's plenty of time to do that later on a phone call with the people you *really want* to do business with. Instead, I like to take my time and learn what others are doing with their businesses.

I don't want to pitch myself uselessly. Besides, most people want to talk about themselves so this is your opportunity to listen. What they don't expect is for you to give them the opportunity to speak, which is refreshing and people will remember that about you.

Besides, you WANT to know what's going on in other people's worlds, right? The information could be useful. You might be surprised to find out — *"Gee, I'm really glad I didn't go first (and tell my story). There's no way, I'd work with this person ...",* or simply, *"I'm glad I didn't waste time talking about me, this person has no clue what I do and couldn't really help me, anyway. Instead, I listened to them! I found out what they do, and that time was spent well. I learned a little and I played myself down; so as not to waste time telling my story to the wrong person. They got to practice their pitch, and I'm glad for that. Next!"*

While you approach people in this manner, you are perceived as someone who really does care about others. You make no judgments and have no preconceived notions. Be positive and encouraging to the person you're listening to.

It's important that you might be able to give business to other attendees and solve some of their problems at the same time. The event, however, can be a great place to find accountants, printers, salespeople, and other representatives for your business by paying attention to what others have to share.

Listen more, and talk less. Save talking about yourself for when there's a **group** of people who want to meet you and you're ready to share your story with as many as you can.

In the meantime, find one thing that you learned from their story, and play it back to them. *"Wow, I never knew that you expanded your company nationwide ... tell me more about that. May I have your business card? I'm definitely going to call you!"* This is called "channeling" — using their words to keep the conversation connected and on track. It establishes comfort and ease.

NETWORKING GOAL #3:
HANDOUTS, FLYERS, POSTCARDS, GIFTS, AUDIO/VIDEO & OTHER GIVEAWAYS!

This is a must. A good marketing plan is the key to making sales. Give out freebies, gifts, press releases, promotional materials, and offer a few pages of your new book to publicize yourself so people won't forget who you are.

Depending on the kind of event you attend, you might want to plan to take along the following:

• **BUSINESS CARDS** (a qualifying must). Get them printed online for FREE at VistaPrint.com or, my favorite, **GotPrint. com**. You don't necessarily have to give them to everyone; in fact, I suggest you hold your cards for those you really want to work with. Give them out discreetly. Have a picture on your card or an image of your product, book, etc. Have a call-to-action message on your card such as *"Sign up for a free (offer/ giveaway) at my website!"* You could put this call-to-action on the back of your business card.

• **FLYERS** for your products, services, seminar announcement, new book, excerpts of your book on single sheets of paper, etc. are a must. You won't have time to tell your whole story, so let people read it when they get home. Plus, you can spare telling your whole story by saying, *"Here's some information about what I do. If like what you read, let's do business! Do you have a card?"*

• **PRESS RELEASE** print-outs are also recommended for every book you've written or businesses that you own and want to promote. If you're going to a media networking party where radio/TV talk show hosts are gathered to meet you and other potential guests, be prepared! Make multiple copies of your press releases to distribute so they don't have to go to your website and read it a week later. If they read your press releases while you're networking with others, they might walk up to you later and say, *"Hey, I enjoyed reading about your successes. Can we book a time when you can be on my show?"* Your response might be, *"Absolutely! What dates and times are good for you?"* Give them a choice of one or two dates and times to quickly nail the appointment.

• **VIDEO/AUDIO LINKS** (i.e., article/book/eBook excerpt recordings, a collection of talk show interviews, sample seminar recordings, etc.). Giving away 5-30 minutes of audio (or video) is a great marketing technique, because after the event, when people are driving home, they can listen to you in audio format! They just met you and they want to hear learn more about you and your business. If you have them, give them an audio CD of you speaking on your favorite business topics, or a link of that same audio online. On the way home, this potential customer can listen to what you have to say/offer. Even a sample of a radio interview might inspire a call or connection to do some business together. Another great reason for promoting audio/video as a handout is to provide more details about your business and possibly answer questions there may not have been time to ask. Seize the opportunity to recommend how you might do some business together that could benefit you both. Practice how you will present yourself to ensure that you are conveying your message in the most powerful and compelling way.

NETWORKING GOAL #4: NEW FANS, LEADS, AFFILIATES, CLIENTS & CUSTOMERS

We network to make more money. It's that simple. You've made your entrance, made a good impression, established yourself and now it's time to make your next move. By showing up in celebrity-fashion with cameras and flashes, and taking a key interest in the lives of others, inevitably, people are going to turn into one of the following: a fan, an affiliate or a customer!

• **FANS** are created when they find out what you do, tell their friends about you, and offer to patronize you to their list of influencers.

• **LEADS** are everywhere. You just have to look for them. They are friends and family, people you just met, and those you have yet to meet. Become a lead magnet for your business and for others. Learn what everyone does so you can leave the event with leads for your own business and leads for your friends and associates. One solid lead for any company can make a big difference in a bottom line. *"George, I've got a lead for you. I just met Susan. She can help you with getting into Company XYZ."*

• **AFFILIATES** are people who find out what you do and how they can help you make money while earning a commission for referrals based on sales. Get their name(s) and contact information and sign these people up as an affiliate (for them) before they do! If you don't have an affiliate program, I recommend it. It means more business for you.

• **CLIENTS & CUSTOMERS** can also pop out of nowhere when networking. Be prepared to make sales. Always be prepared with order forms and a few payment processing methods for the customer that wants to place an order on the spot.

Not every networking event delivers the same results every time. People are different and so are their environment, business climate, circumstances as well as what's happening in your life or business. These events allow you to collect worthy information about current and future trends and possibly give you a leg up on your competition. While you may not generate a lot of leads at one networking event, you may pick up a few useful nuggets of data that you can actually use.

NETWORKING GOAL #5:
SALES! SALES! SALES! SALES!

YES, it is *possible* to make *"sales on the spot"* when you're networking, especially if you happen to have your books, audio programs or other products on hand for people to check out.

ReallyFastBooks.com | SpeakerCafe.com | TVGuest.com

I remember going to a networking event where I carried two books that I authored. People were genuinely curious. It provided a natural opening to talk about my work.

I was able to talk to them while they held my books in their hands. When soon-to-be customers can hold something tangible, they make a personal connection to you and your product. It begs the question you want to hear, *"Are your books for sale? How much? Can I write you a check? I have cash too ..."* You can confidently respond with, "Sure, they're only $____." Then, don't forget to autograph the book for them. You might also offer a discount.

When other people see you selling your book(s) and autographing them, what do you think is going through their mind? You guessed it! They're going to get in line to buy your book, too! Don't get overly excited no matter how many people rush to buy your book/product from you. Stay cool and confident.

Keep your earnings organized and on your mind throughout the event. You might just end up making a lot of sales and a lot of money. Don't lose track of sales. It can get chaotic when people start approaching you to ask questions and making purchases. This is where a trustworthy ally comes in handy to assist you with sales. You do the talking and the autographing while your helper handles the administrative details.

When autographing books, ask buyers to complete a small order form (if you have one) with their names and contact information so you can contact them later with special deals or updates. Think of the *potential income* from returning customers!

So, after they've filled in their small order form, and you've autographed their book, ask for a photo, *"Can I get a picture with you? I'll send it to you via eMail if you like ..."* Who will resist an offer like that? There you have it ... more happy customers to showcase on your website.

Networking should focus the attention on growing your business and developing two-way dialogues that have benefits to all parties involved. The important thing to remember about networking is the growth you will experience by putting yourself "out there" and taking steps to improve yourself and your business. Now, let's continue ... there's more to learn!

NETWORKING GOAL #6:
THANK YOU, GOOD NIGHT & RE-INVITES!

Very often, when I am out networking, I'm usually the last one to leave these events. Often times, I've even offered to help the event host, meeting planner or speakers close down. I've even helped them transfer materials to their cars, folded up banners, collected pens and flyers, and made myself useful. This is why.

You see, besides saying, *"Good night and thank you for the invitation ..."*, hosts and speakers get a kick out of those who stay the extra 5-10 minutes after the presentation. People begin to wind down, reflect on the event, and share some of their own views as to how things went. They also ask YOU for your opinion and then they listen ... INTENTLY ... particularly if the feedback is constructive, something they can use to improve the performance. This is a choice opportunity to really make a lasting impression and learn something.

Now, you would never be required to stay after a meeting, particularly to wrap up. But, try it some time. Especially, when you're the main attraction or people just enjoy talking to you. Stick around and make yourself useful. That's how you create fans, affiliates and clients. By taking just an extra 5, 10, 15, or 20 minutes to help others.

When it comes to saying, "goodnight" and "goodbye," remember to thank the speaker personally with a hand shake, a smile and a photograph (if possible). Thank the manager of the restaurant, event coordinator for the hotel banquet room, speakers and staff. Everyone is a potential contact and if the event was successful, they certainly deserve your appreciation, especially, if it is your event.

With the contacts you make at networking events, anything can happen. You may be solicited to speak, MC, or host another event. You might be asked to participate as a guest on a radio show or get interviewed for their newsletter or online eZine. That's the "magic" of networking!

Be yourself, professional, and generally interested. People can tell very quickly if you are the real deal! In my experience, I've never seen anything less than what I've just described happen to me. These experiences have proven to be very successful.

NETWORKING GOAL #7:
EXPAND FOR NEW GROWTH
FOR MORE BUSINESS!

The final goal I want to accomplish when I network after photographs, introductions, passing out my marketing literature, audio/video samples and business cards, while making sales, developing new fans, leads and affiliates, saying my and getting invited back to the next networking event ... is to expand my business for new growth, sales, branding and goodwill. This *is* the ultimate goal!

Everything you do at a networking event should about developing customers and new leads to consistently grow and expand your business. Period!

In the sections ahead, we'll go over what to say, what to wear, what to bring, what to ask, what not to ask, etc. We'll also go into more detail regarding these goals so you better understand what it takes to be a master networker.

NETWORKING COMPONENT #4

TOOLS

Know What Tools You Need To Effectively Network With Others!

In order to be truly successful at networking, you'll need more than just a business card, if you even have them or use them. What's more valuable these days is to know what tools you can utilize (both online and offline) to maximize your networking success.

In this section, you will learn about a handful of tools you can use to effectively start, grow and manage your network of prospects, clients, vendors and affiliates. Having the right tools will allow you to keep track of all the people you initially connected with and plan to communicate with and more.

To be a highly-effective networker, you should have (potentially) *all* of these suggested tools in place before you head out to network in order to make the most out of meeting people for business, making money and helping others do the same!

Understand that networking is not so much about self-promotion as it is about developing and maintaining mutually beneficial relationships with all of your contacts. The tips that follow will help you to become a master networker.

"ONLINE" NETWORKING TOOLS

- **WEBSITE** - Your website should be designed to provide more information about you and what you do. Don't have one? Get one built for you or learn to build one yourself using some of the online self-building website solutions such as SquareSpace.com, Wix.com and Weebly.com. You could also just build a Facebook Fan Page and use that as your website.

- **FACEBOOK FAN PAGE/GROUP** - I mentioned this in an earlier section. These are great Facebook tools you can use when attracting people your way at a networking event offline or attracting people online to you. Don't have a fan page or group? Build one or start one!

- **CRM (CONTACT DATABASE)** - Depending on your budget and the ultimate purpose of your contact management system, you might choose to use something as simple as **Google Contacts** or step it up a notch with **Marketing360.com**, **Zoho.com/crm**, HubSpot CRM, SalesForce.com, Close.io, ClinchPad, Pipedrive, Prosperworks, PipelineDeals, Pipeliner, SugarCRM, Podio, Odoo, and TrackVia.

- **CALENDAR SYSTEM** - While there are several calendar systems at your disposal, two of them come to mind: **Google Calendar** (for simplicity) and **Calendly.com**, which allows people to book time with you. Create a memorable user name, such as Calendly.com/*bookyourfirstname*. That way, you can text people that simple URL to their phone so they can book time with you quickly and easily.

- **FILMORA** - Video editing software for sprucing up your recorded videos of the event you just attended last night. You can learn more about it at **Filmora.WonderShare.com**.

- **VIDEO SHARING WEBSITE ACCOUNTS** - Once you have your video all spruced up, you can upload it to your video sharing accounts at these websites: **YouTube.com**, **Instagram.com**, **Vube.com**, **DailyMotion.com**, **Vimeo.com**, **SlideShare.net**, among others out there. Once the event is over, if you recorded any video of the event (with you in it, preferably), upload it to these websites.

- **PODCASTING SOFTWARE** - After the event, you might talk about the highlights and who you met on your podcast show. You might even interview someone you met. To create your own podcast show, all you need is an account at **Libsyn.com** or **SoundCloud.com**. Once you upload your show's recording, you can submit your audio links to iTunes and other podcasting website submission sites.

- **WEBINAR SOFTWARE** - You can easily convert newly met people into contacts on your eMail list if you announce you conduct educational and informative webinars every once in awhile. "Would you like to be notified when I give a live training online via webinar? Great, just enter your name/ eMail and phone number on this list to be notified." For this, you can use **WebinarJam.com** or **EasyWebinar.com** software.

- **TELE-SEMINAR SERVICES** - If you conduct tele-seminars similarly to how you would conduct webinars, you can make the same "get on my list" offer to be notified. For this, you might use **ConferenceCalling.com** or **ConferenceCall.com**.

- **VIDEO CONFERENCING** - After you attend an event, you might want to conduct a one-on-one video conferencing session with an attendee you just met. To do this, you could use **Zoom.us** or **Google Duo** (app) on your phone.

- **SOCIAL MEDIA MANAGEMENT TOOLS** - Tools such as **SocialOomph.com**, AgoraPulse.com (Simple & Affordable Social Media Management), **Hootsuite.com**, Buffer.com, **SproutSocial.com**, Tailwind.com, IFTTT.com, Tweepi.com, HeyOrca.com, Socedo.com, Post66.com, Brand24.com, NapoleonCat.com, Falcon.io, Social Daddy, SocialPilot.com, TweepleSearch.com, SocialReport.comm, among others.

"OFFLINE" NETWORKING TOOLS

- **BUSINESS CARDS** - Optional, unless you like using them as throw-away promotional cards to showcase a product, book or service you have. Sure, put your phone number and website on them. Otherwise, most people just enter their phone number into the other person's phone to save time, paper and expense in purchasing business cards. If you do have business cards, put your photo on them so people remember who you are when they see your business card after the event. Also, put special offers and a call-to-action or two on your card. Just don't list your name, title, address, phone number, website and eMail address. You might also put your Skype handle and other social media links on there as well, if you have business cards printed. Also, make use of both sides of the business card. You can document a list of your products and services on the back side of the card. You could also provide all of your websites on the back of your cards. Cards can help drive traffic to your sites and interest in what you have to offer because people can find you on the Web! In lieu of handing out your business cards, you might just have a large-size image of your business card, front and back, in JPG form to text someone. They'll never lose it! ;-) Plus, have them take a picture of you on the spot so they associate who that business card belongs to. Of course, when you get home, enter the contact information from those business cards you collected into your contact management system, either by scanning them in or entering them by hand. Once that's done, toss the cards or keep a few that caught your attention from a design point of view. For business cards, I get mine printed at **GotPrint.com.**

- **POSTCARDS** – Depending on what you have to sell, promote, advertise, announce, you might get postcards made to do just that when you attend networking events. You can get upwards of 500 postcards printed for around $20 at places like **GotPrint.com**. Search online for the best deal, of course.

- **FLYERS** – Another useful tool when promoting whatever it is you want to promote. You can design full-page flyers, 1/2 page fliers, 1/4 page flyers, double-sided or single-sided flyers. It's up to you and what you need to promote. You might also consider black and white printing versus color printed fyers. For full-color flyers, check out **BestValueCopy.com** for their great low prices.

- **NAME/EMAIL SHEET + CLIPBOARD** – This is an easy way to build your list. Without it, your list will grow slowly, if at all, when only adding 1-3 contacts per event you attend. The idea here is this, attach a prize or giveaway to the name/email list. "I'm giving away one of my books and a few other prizes. Simply enter your name, phone number and eMail address to win a chance at one of the prizes." Done. At the end of the night, you have a nice size list, a few happy winners, and a reason to reach out to everyone on your list again in the future. "Hey, I decided to let all the other people on the list win something too. I'm giving you free access to my book/audio online in digitial format. Just follow this link to register and you're in! Great meeting you the other night. Let's catch up when you have time!"

- **SAMPLE PRODUCT, BOOKS, ETC.** - What do you sell? Can you bring those samples with you? Did you write a book? Bring a few copies with you. You're bound to sell a copy or two, or at least take a photos of people holding your book. Especially if they're one of your winners.

- **RECOMMENDED RESOURCES ONE-SHEET** – Depending on the type of event you're attending, you could create a one-sheet (single or double-sided) with a list of recommended resources, website links, vendors and/or service providers that you use and can recommend to others. This is a great handout idea, because people will appreciate the referrals, the time you took to think of them (in this manner) and, in turn, they'll remember you because your contact information is printed on this one-sheet. You could also send them a link to this very page online if you can get their eMail address. If you're recommending products/services where you potentially receive a referral commission from any of the vendors on your one-sheet, you might make a statement like, "Mention My Name _____" when contacting your vendors for __% off, if such discounts are available. Either way, you want to be sure you get credit.

- **CELL PHONE** – Never leave home without it, right? Granted, while your ringer is turned off (or on vibrate) while you network, use your phone to the max! Take pictures and/or record video of the event and who you meet. Take pictures of the building if it's a nice hotel, of the sign outside the door where you're going to network if there is one, a picture of the room with all the people, etc.

- **TABLET** – If you have one, it can come in handy when you want people to enter their name and contact information into your database for you. Plus, it's exciting for them to do so when you say you'll be giving away any number of random prize drawings at the end of the night. Makes you look official and you're not even hosting the event!

- **POINT-OF-PURCHASE CREDIT CARD PROCESSING DEVICE** - If you plan on making sales at the event, don't forget to bring your SQUARE or PAYPAL credit card charging device to take credit card payments on the spot. Otherwise, print order forms to take with you. People can enter their credit card information on the form and you can then process their order when you get home. Be sure you can read their handwriting and proof-read their credit card number and their telephone number back to them to be sure everything was entered correctly on the order form. If you don't have one of these devices, you can easily download Cash.me or Venmo (app) to your mobile phone. These apps allow people to push money to you. Once they push the instructed dollar amount to you, you can then transfer those monies to your bank account. Done. You got paid!

- **ORDER FORMS** - I just mentioned this. Don't leave home without them too. You never know if someone or a group of people are going to order something from you at the networking event. Don't be caught without them. That's like leaving money on the table. Shame on you!

- **NAMETAG** – You might goes as far as to create your own professional-looking nametag with your name and business logo on it. Why not? It's a very inexpensive investment because it can be re-used again and again at different networking events. The next time you show up to an event, your custom-made nametag will look impressive. The more professional you appear, the more people will notice you and ultimately want to talk to you!

Here are a few more tips to consider when designing your own nametag: [1] Make sure people can read it from a distance of about 10 feet. [2] Use a first name or nickname on the nametag and last name. [3] Add your website address.

Make your nametag on your computer using any word processing program. Print and cut to slide it into a nametag holder (bought at any office supply store). Wear the tag on the left side so you do not cover it when shaking hands.

If name tags are pre-made for you for pick up at the event, **sign your name** if there's room. I do! If the name tag simply states "Hello," write your name on it. Don't let the host or attendant write your name. YOU WRITE IT and don't use cursive. Print in ALL CAPS. It's easier to read for people to read your name.

• **LAPTOP** – Usually a cell phone and/or tablet can do the job of a laptop when networking, but the only reason to possibly bring a laptop is if you plan on showcasing something online that you might like a larger screen to do so. Such as, I have a 17" laptop monitor that makes my cookies jump out at you when you walk by my table (if I have one) at any networking event. You might also transact sales in real-time using your laptop, if you don't have such capabilities on your phone or tablet. It's up to you. Otherwise, leave the laptop at home or in the trunk of your car for safekeeping.

• **VIDEO CAMERA** – While cell phones have cameras built into them for taking great photos and video, perhaps, you'd like the enhanced capabilities that go along with a real video camera (with built-in photo-taking capabilities. I still like to take a digital/video camera with me whenever I go networking. These days, many of the cameras have wifi capabilities that allow you to send those high-quality photos to your phone or social media sharing website. Pretty cool! Remember to take pictures with the attendees, hosts, speakers and others at every networking event. Post photos on your website in your press room. Take pictures of the meeting place where the event took place. Consider creating a virtual tour of the event to show people where you've been. Your tour could include pictures of the building's entrance, building signs, lobby area, meeting area, event sign, etc. Record the event with you as the virtual host on video and share your video online.

• **HELP** – Consider having someone come with you and follow you around at a networking event and ask them to digitally record the meeting and you shaking hands with people you meet. Upload those photos and video of the event to your website or social website accounts as soon as you get home! ALWAYS WATCH

YOUR EQUIPMENT. Keep your camera in your hands, in your bag, or with someone you trust. Lock equipment in the trunk of your car out of sight. Trust no one! Suspect everyone!

- **REFERRAL BUSINESS CARDS** – These cards belong to friends and business acquaintances you know and trust. When you meet someone you can't help, you may know someone who can. It's also a good idea to write on the back of each card, "Referred by YOUR NAME" so that the person remembers you, and mentions your name to their business call for help. Do your best to make arrangements with these businesses. There could be potential for investment or commission representing them.

- **BOOKS, PRODUCT SAMPLES, USB DRIVE GIVEAWAYS, ETC.** – While these products might not be tools, in the usual definition, they can be used as tools to help promote what you do and impress people. Be sure to bring them along. Even if you just keep them in the car, they're available and quickly accessible when you want to show someone something you've created, authored, etc.

- **CARRY-ON LUGGAGE BAG (WITH WHEELS)** – For the professional networker who has a lot to transport to an event, such as product samples, books, product inventory to sell (or show), consider professional looking, roller carry-on bag. You know this will come in handy if you plan to sell your books or other materials. It could be your store on wheels! "Cha-Ching!"

- **PRESS RELEASES** – Bring them to the events, especially if you're going to a networking event where you know people from the media, talks show hosts, show producers, agents, scouts, publicity folk, etc. that may be prospecting for their shows. With your press release in hand, you can give it to them personally. They can read it when they have down time during an event. If you are unable to make another connection, you will want to follow up with that person by phone or eMail. On the other hand, one of them might walk up to you and comment, "Wow, I just read your press release while I was having lunch. I'd like to have you as a guest on my radio program. When can we talk?"

• **<u>FOOD, CANDY, GUM, MINTS, ETC.</u>** – Many people are grateful if you offer them gum, mint or some kind of food/candy at an event. I always keep a pack of ORBIT "Wintergreen" flavored gum on me. I offer it as an ice breaker. I remember one event someone wanted everyone to hand out our business cards. I didn't have a card. I had gum though. Guess who everyone remembered when that activity was over? You bet, ME! "The gum guy!" Funny as it may seem, I also bring my world famous chocolate chip cookies. Again, I steal the show with them every time. So, consider bringing something small, easy to transport, something most everyone will enjoy or find thoughtful.

NETWORKING COMPONENT #5

RESOURCES

Always Come Prepared!

When networking with others, be prepared to provide any number of (online or offline) business or personal resources designed to help others and their business.

One of the hardest aspects for getting any business off the ground is locating the right resources to help you in the areas where you need the most help.

> One of the biggest assets you have when you walk into any room to network will be your own pool of personal and professional resources. Share these with others. Assist them with solutions or give them a resource referral. Referrals can be very lucrative. Inquire about commissions if it seems appropriate.

Taking the time to invest in quality business and personal resources is just another way for you to earn at a networking event! Who says you can't make money networking?

Types Of Businesses You Need To Know & Have Ready To Refer When The Opportunity Presents Itself

Professionals in your field may be people you do not directly work with, but who share the same passions or career choice. These are people you can refer business (services) to. Frequently, these referrals generate commissions that pay a one-time fee or ongoing residual income depending on the type of business service you refer.

Suppliers you do business with might need *your* services. Refer your clients and those you meet to your suppliers and collect a commission or a discount off the services they provide. For example, I referred so much business to a particular service provider that I was never charged for the services I used. I even received free accounts saving me hundreds of dollars per month.

It's important to remember, commissions and dividends don't always come in the form of cash payments. They sometimes come in the form of services, which have their own cash value. Over time, the value of these services can be quite substantial.

Perhaps, they're services you need. You might opt to receive the services in exchange for referrals or services you can provide the vendor. While it isn't cash *in your pocket*, exchanging services *saves you money.*

Clients: Ideally, you have built up a relationship of trust with your clients. Some may be able to assist you in other ways such as suppliers, supporters and referrals. When you can help someone earn a commission, it adds more than cash to your bottom line.

Co-Workers: Typically, one will spend more waking hours with co-workers versus family or friends. Ask for referrals to dentists, doctors, contractors, mechanics, attorneys, locksmiths, etc. See how your networking world is continually evolving?

Clubs or Association Members: If you are involved with any community, professional associations or activities, you have a ready-made network. Most people join these groups to meet others. The door is already open. Refer businesses and personal service providers to them.

Volunteer Groups: One of the more primary reasons people volunteer is to meet others and to feel a part of something bigger than themselves. Get to know your fellow volunteers. Refer who you know (businesses and personal service providers) to them. Keep networking!

Acquaintances: You meet dozens of people in work and social settings. Don't waste these opportunities to learn more about them. Friendships often start out this way. Great networks thrive this way!

Micro-Newsletters: Print a small newsletter about your business to distribute. Some prospects will be genuinely interested in having more information about you. It should be professional and newsworthy only. On the back, provide a list of helpful resources you can recommend. Provide their website, telephone number, contact information and a short description of their services.

Referral Business Cards: Carry the cards for businesses you know and trust. When meeting someone for the first time, give them a card! It's a good idea to write on the back of each card, "Referred by your name" so that the person remembers you and mentions you to the business. You always get back what you give out, so make sure you refer people that deserve the promotion.

Other Networking Cards: It can be very helpful to carry a few 3 x 5 cards to explain what you do. This is especially suitable for businesses that often have complicated terms or concepts. Provide definitions for those terms as well as a means to learn more.

Key People: When emergencies strike and you need help, or someone you meet needs help, it is good to have a list of key contacts you know and trust. Nurture these relationships by sending greeting cards, having lunch and contacting them, periodically, in person or over the telephone.

This is important! Some of the key people you should have in your repertoire might be:

1. Accountants/Tax Preparers	8. Locksmiths
2. Computer Repair Experts	9. Mechanics
3. Dentist/Doctors	10. Publicists
4. Graphic Designers	11. Vendors/Suppliers
5. Hair Stylists	12. Video/Audio Experts
6. Investors/Fundraisers	13. Virtual Assistants
7. Lawyers/Attorneys	14. Webmasters

Keep these names and telephone numbers handy and be ready to refer new business to them whenever someone says,

"Do you know of a good accountant?" You will be prepared to say, *"I certainly do, call my good friend _____?"*

Let's face it, most of us are either too passive or too aggressive in our business life, and we end up never getting the support, recognition, or respect that we want and need. These are challenges everyone faces so when we can help each other, we feel empowered ... that anything is possible.

RECOMMENDED RESOURCE LINKS

Do you have a list of recommended resources links on your website? Why not create a one-sheet with some of the top 10 or 21 resources you recommend? Then, offer to hand them out to people who might find them valuable.

I've done this in the past and people really appreciate the time and effort you put into something like this. Plus, they save so much time looking for resources they never knew exhisted until you shared them.

Make a list of all the companies, software, supplies, vendors and other resources you use that might be helpful to others if they had that list.

What Can You Add To The List Above?

The effectiveness of each resource will vary depending on the way you use it in business as well as your knowledge of the resource.

With regard to your pool of resources, vendors, and service providers, who do you know that you can recommend to all the new people you plan to meet at networking events? Generate a good list of your "people" and hand it out. What a gift and a time-saver for anyone who needs a referral.

By offering something tangible, information worth keeping, people will remember you, in addition to the business card and a handshake. Most people will appreciate receiving lists of new services that they can actually take depend on. Is your list ready?

NETWORKING
COMPONENT #6

PREPARATION

Preparation is all about the THREE Rs:
RESEARCH ▶ REHEARSE ▶ REVIEW

Research the companies that might be represented at your networking event. Research the company leaders, services, products and their competition.

REHEARSE WHAT YOU WILL SAY. Research the people you intend to meet. Make a list of questions if needed. Don't miss opportunities to learn and do some business at the same time.

WHAT WILL YOU TAKE to the networking event and what will you wear? Make no assumptions about how much time this might take. Plan a few days ahead of the event to ensure you know what the dress code is and have time to prepare the materials you should take with you.

"FIRST IMPRESSIONS" ARE SO IMPORTANT at networking events. At the last minute or even a couple hours before the event is *not* the time to start worrying about your dry cleaning or making copies of flyers, handouts, postcards, invitations, etc., to distribute at the event.

Start creating your flyers and preparing your handouts days/weeks in advance of the event. You'll be glad you gave yourself the extra time to work on these projects so you are ready to make an entrance.

RESEARCH THE COMPANY that is sponsoring the networking event you're attending by visiting their website. Scan through their entire website including the press room. Read their ABOUT US page, any articles/press releases, blog, etc. How often do they host networking events? What's the average attendance? Do they hire speakers? Could you be one?

LISTEN TO AUDIO CLIPS, PODCAST SHOWS, AND/OR VIDEOS on their website or YouTube.com channel if they have one available.

WHO WORKS FOR THE COMPANY? Write their names down so you know who to ask when you arrive at the event. Prepare by reading biographies and other information on their website before attending the event.

AS A CONVERSATION STARTER, refer to something you liked or learned from their website. Such as, *"I was on your website last night, and I noticed _____. Can you tell me more about that?"* Do your homework on people, the group or company. You never know when you're going to meet the PRESIDENT of the company or the facilitator on the way to the rest room.

Have something prepared, noteworthy and positive to say about their company, product line, successes, even their competition. Impress them with what your knowledge of the company and the industry.

PRACTICE AND REHEARSE WHAT YOU'LL SAY. Formulate the specific points you want to make and know the questions you want to ask. It proves your level of interest and understanding of their business, which they will appreciate.

WHAT WILL YOU BRING TO THE NETWORKING EVENT? Will the media attend this function? Will they be looking for potential guests for their shows such as you? Are you prepared to sell yourself? Bring copies of your press releases, audio/video samples (on a USB drive, optional) as a take-away. If you've authored any books, have copies that you can give to these media decision-makers. Know who will be attending. Sometimes, you can get a list of attendees in advance from the host company. Be prepared.

DEVELOP A BRIEF INTRODUCTION. Do you have any new products or services you'd like to include in your revised "elevator speech?" When introducing yourself, you have about 15-30 seconds to make that first impression. Getting attention is one thing; maintaining it is quite another.

The introduction should identify what you do and with whom you are associated (company, business partner, etc.)

> **"I work with** commercial artists (company/business name) **helping them to** increase their sales and profits."

This introduction should encourage the others to ask for more information. When they do, recite the 30-second presentation that you prepared and support it with a few details:

"For example, XYZ Company was looking for a way to increase their sales online. After working with them for a few months on their selling practices, we realized an increase in sales by 80%! By increasing the number of products they sell, we also increased their net earnings by 95% I suppose you could say that I help people make more money!"

Every introduction needs to be well-rehearsed so you can confidently articulate your message any time and under any circumstance. Use actual case studies to educate your audience. Include lessons in your presentation and ideas for the others to consider.

It is better to be active in one professional association then to periodically attend meetings of many. Once you become an active member, people will start to recognize you, view you as a colleague and trust you.

EDUCATE YOURSELF – Read everything about your industry to augment your knowledge and to improve your skill base such as trade journals, magazines, websites, eZines, newsletters, etc.

CAMERA – Never attend a networking event without a digital camera, whether it's on your phone, a digital video camera, etc. Be prepared to photograph the event coordinator(s), guest speaker(s), and other respected guests. This gives you an excellent marketing advantage for your website. Get their names and their website addresses, too.

Be sure to tell your new contacts to check out your website (or social networking sites) in a few days to view photographs from the event. Encourage them to download them to their website (or social pages). Ask them to place a description to identify who's in the photo. Imagine the increase visibility when others are showcasing your photo in their press rooms! Make it easy for them to promote you and share your products/services with their audience.

PRODUCT PRESENTATIONS – You never know when you may

be asked to put on a product demonstration or demonstrate a particular service, audio recording, website tour, client portfolio, book cover design, etc. This would be a good time to break out the new book you just wrote or play your audio program on their phones, iPads, iPods, or portable MP3 players. If you take your laptop or iPad to an event for a presentation, to display catalog items or use charts and graphs, keep your laptop or iPad with you all times. Be prepared to make impromptu product or service presentations about what you do in the event someone asks.

GUEST LIST – When possible, obtain a list of guests prior to an event so you know who will be attending. This will give you time to research attendees and the companies they represent. Google will enable you to learn just about everything you will need to feel well-informed when meeting others for the first time. Guest lists can help you identify those you especially want to meet. It is good to know this before you walk through the door. You can generally get this data from the event host. At a minimum, you should know the type of event that you are attending (small business people, systems people, rocket scientists, etc.). Perhaps, there is an R.S.V.P. list you can access.

FIND OUT WHAT THE PARKING SITUATION IS LIKE AT THE EVENT. Ask the event coordinator or call the property manager where the event will be held. Sometimes, the website for this event or a flyer will provide information. Why is this important?

- **Street parking?** You may need to have coins. Keep $5-$10 in quarters, dimes and nickels in your car at all times. Check the meter often unless you are good for 12 hours. After 6:00 P.M., it's usually free. But, read the meter to be sure. You might also keep $5-$10 in quarters in your briefcase or purse for unplanned "parking" situations.

- **Residential?** Watch out for parking after 6:00 P.M. in certain parts of the city. Look for NO PARKING AFTER __:__ __ P.M. signs or you might get TICKETED or worse ... TOWED!

- **Covered parking?** Bring CASH! Keep at least $20-$40 in

cash to pay for covered parking unless cards are accepted.

TAKE A CHANGE OF CLOTHES WITH YOU. You never know when you'll be invited to go out dancing, for drinks, to run, jog, walk along the beach or a hiking trail, etc. Men, you may wish to have a clean shirt in your briefcase for a number of reasons. Ladies, what would you do if coffee were to spill on your skirt or slacks? Always be prepared.

CLEAN YOUR CAR (INSIDE AND OUT) BEFORE YOU GO TO A NETWORKING EVENT. SAMPLE SCENARIO: You're getting along famously with the new group of people you just and everyone embraces your idea to have dinner and drinks after the event. You then remember the dog hair all over the seats of your car and the running shoes you meant to throw in the washing machine. This is why a clean car, inside and out, will make another good impression of how you take care of your personal property.

For your own protection, limit alcohol intake and if you are the designated driver, don't take any chances with your life or that of your colleagues. If you want to make another good impression, remain sober. If things get rowdy, you could learn a lot about the people that are working the dance floor and Jim Beam.

PLACE ALL OF YOUR VALUABLES IN THE TRUNK OF YOUR CAR. Hide your briefcases, purses, wallets, and other valuables, in the trunk. Leave nothing inside your car that might attract the wrong kind of attention. Keep a blanket in your car if you want to cover up stuff in the backseat.

CAR SECURITY – Do you have AAA? Suppose you are the last person to leave the event and the only person in the parking lot when you notice that you've locked your keys in the car. Do you know any friendly mechanics in the area working late? NO! With roadside coverage, such as AAA, is a phone call away. Their membership pays for itself, as you get a number of discounts from hotels, car-rentals, travel and even purchases at popular stores.

PREPARE YOUR CAR THE DAY BEFORE. Make sure the gas tank is full prior to driving to an event; wash your car windows; clean your car (inside and out); check the oil, radiator fluid, coolant ... I'm not kidding! Don't risk the chance of your car breaking down and missing an important event for something you neglected to do such as fill up. Few gas stations are open all night as well as stores and restaurants. Do you have a spare tire/kit and jumper cables? Always be prepared.

SUPPLY YOUR CAR WITH GUM, MINTS, CELL PHONE (WALL) CHARGER, WATER BOTTLES, handy-wipes, napkins, fruit (for a long drive), etc.

USE GPS OR GOOGLE® MAP SYSTEM to get directions to an event prior to departure. You know you won't be late when you can find alternative routes when the freeway is bumper-to-bumper. Your cell phone should be equipped with a GPS tracking system if your car does not ... no excuses for getting lost.

EDUCATION – Read, read, read everything you can to build knowledge and skill base. Read trade journals for your business industry. There's nothing worse than listening to an innovative speaker when you don't comprehend what's being said because you didn't do your homework or haven't kept up with the world.

KEEP HEALTHY AND FIT! Work out at least every other day and stay in great shape! It's good for your body and it's good for your peace of mind! Eat right and don't overindulge when out with others. This doesn't mean that you can't spoil yourself with food and drink once in awhile. Overall, stay strong; eat light; drink light. Bad habits can be very offensive. Think about the impression you are making.

INVENTORY – Keep plenty of books, audio, products, flyers, business cards, etc., in the trunk of your car for a little "show and tell" when you arrive at an event. You might be in a conversation with someone when you think of a book you just read, that you'd like to share ... and you happen to have a copy of it in your car. I've been known to pack a box of office products, books, binders, spirals, and more. I'm prepared for anything! I enjoy hearing statements such as, *"Wow, this guy knows his stuff. What's the title of the book you read on marketing myths? I could use that information! Thanks for the great tip, Bart!"*

GET PUMPED – LISTEN TO UPBEAT MUSIC RIGHT BEFORE GOING INTO THE EVENT. Music is a powerful force and can produce a high level of energy for inspiration. Music can inspire higher brain functioning and creativity. Personally, I listen to my favorite tunes in the car on the way to most events. By the time arrive at my event, I'm charged! People pick up on it, too. They notice your vitality and decide that they definitely want to talk to you. So, whether you prefer classical rock to Iron Maiden, let it energize you and work the magic, calm the nerves and intensify your good mood.

DO YOU HAVE AN AFFILIATE PROGRAM? DON'T MISS THIS. Let's say you meet someone really interested in selling your products to their list of clients and subscribers. You REALLY want to MAKE SURE they get signed up? Their huge list translates to money in the bank for you and for them. You want to have access to their list ASAP. Time is money so don't waste it. Reassure your new affiliate that you can make this happen and you look forward to issuing commissions to him/her every month.

Advisedly, tell them, *"I'll get you signed up and eMail all the information you need to start marketing to your list and earning commissions immediately. I don't want you to lift a finger! If you have any questions, after I send you the information, just let me know. Thanks!"* You make it easy for the affiliates to make money, they will come!

You should be feeling on top of the world too, because you just secured an affiliate who's only going to focus on marketing for you. You're going to help them get started and it becomes a win-win for both of you.

Now, if you don't have an affiliate program associated with

your website and the products you sell from it, then there are several ways to acquire one. Visit *MyTrainingCenter.com* for more information about affiliate programs, affiliate marketing and affiliate software. Networking without signing up new affiliates for your website is unproductive and missed opportunity!

NETWORKING ON THE ROAD. Make your list; check it twice. Take products to sell, flyers, postcards, and anything else that will fit in your bag. I prefer to drive to most of my events so I have all the materials/equipment I need when I need it. Otherwise, you are restricted when checking in at the airport. Then, when you consider the time it takes to travel by plane today, you might as well consider driving should you anticipate a layover or delay. Sometimes, it's even more economical to rent a car versus flying if you have concerns about the reliability of your automobile.

WHAT SHOULD YOU WEAR? Men: Shoes polished, sharp belt, sports coat, dry cleaned shirt for a professional image that makes a statement ... Women: Dress appropriately (i.e., business attire) for the event. Walk the talk; dress for success; know the audience you will be networking with.

WHEN ARE GIVING GIFTS APPROPRIATE? Holidays aren't the only time to give gifts. However, knowing when and what is important to know. I gave a business gift one time and it paid off in referrals and sales. My intent was to thank the individual for their efforts in organizing a great event. Whatever you decide to give, quality is essential and the cost should be nominal. Keep it professional. Suggestions could be flowers, a small office plant, a good writing pen, restaurant gift certificate and even a Starbucks card will make some people do the happy dance. A small token of appreciation will speak a thousand words.

HAVE A WEBSITE THAT SELLS YOU! People that you've spoken with on the phone should be looking for you at a networking event. Be prepared to follow up on your conversation, to answer questions, take orders, sign them up as an affiliate, and get all of their business information. Have your FREE offer ready such a newsletter, audio/report, plus much more.

Should You Go It Alone Or Take A Guest With You?

PROS & CONS

Attending (Networking Events) ALONE! = *PROS* ... You can navigate freely throughout the event without concern for the person that (might have) accompanied you to the event. You have the ability to focus on your own agenda, leave when you want to, or join a group of people afterwards for dinner and drinks or just to wrap up a late night conversation.

Attending (Networking Events) ALONE! = *CONS* ... The CONS include not having that edge to walk up to people (individually or in a group) or the visual appearance (of being in a social mood) to attract others to walk up and meet you. Sometimes, it's easier to introduce yourself to strangers when you've got a friend with you by your side to offset everyone's nervousness. Going solo can also make people feel uncomfortable, somewhat shy, or intimitading because they're all alone.

Going WITH OTHERS (to Networking Events) = *PROS* ... You can generate a lot of interest in meeting others when you are part of a group that appears to be having fun, is talkative, and genuinely interested in the meeting other people at the event. Talk about shared energies. It's as easy as, *"Hi, what's your name? These are my friends, Gayl and John. They're in media and seminar sales training. What do you do? Why don't you join us while we move around the room meeting new people."*

Going WITH OTHERS (to Networking Events) = *CONS* ... When you arrive in a group, it can be challenging to leave the group to network if you are more of a soloist and not so dependent on the crowd to support your meeting new people. Traveling in the same car, for example, also requires that everyone be prepared to leave at the same time and doesn't give you the luxury to make plans to continue conversations after the event is over. Circulating can be an issue in a group especially if others seem to be interested in what your company's products/services offer. If you are with a group, it would be a good idea to set up some ground rules and agreement on things like departure time, consensus to leave early if the event proves invaluable, and other factors.

You be the judge for your own needs. Going with one person might be better than attending an event en masse. Driving in separate cars allows your associates to go home when they're ready especially if you've decided to remain at the event until the crowd departs to pick up some inside tips and help out if needed.

LET OTHERS KNOW WHERE YOU'LL BE NETWORKING! Post your appearances at certain events on your website, online calendar, and in your press room, before and after the event! Help others network with you. Take the pressure off them by inviting them to come along. Then, introduce them to others and watch your network grow!

SMALL THINGS THAT ARE USEFUL. You're going to want Chapstick because you will be doing a lot of talking, mints, gum, change, mini-toothbrush and toothpaste, electric shaver (guys), makeup kit (ladies) ... WetOnes® are a great idea considering you'll be shaking a number of hands (or not). Make an effort to wash your hands before the event, during the event and after the event before you get in the car to drive home. Or, keep sanitation lotion in the car so you can clean your hands from all that handshaking.

PREPARE FOR NETWORKING OPPORTUNITIES ALL YEAR LONG! It would be helpful to know which networking events you plan to attend. Choose from a selection of national conventions, trade shows and expos in your industry or competing industries. Some events charge an "admission" fee while others are free.

This would probably be a good time for you to set up a budget for your networking activities. Know your budget. Then organize the events locally and nationally and set aside the funds to attend all of those that will promote you and your business. Many events require that you pay in advance. Most networking events are tax deductible because they are employment-related. Save your receipts. Check with your accountant for details.

Having a detailed budget helps you to think strategically about the types of events you'd like to attend and would best serve your business needs.

Next, plan to attend 1-3 networking events locally. Seize these opportunities to get to know people in your community and the companies and services available to you and your business. Particularly at the local level, you will have many chances to work with others by supporting their endeavors. There will be many moments for you to shine, join local organizations, and become an active participant in your area.

Networking events can also include seminars, workshops, classes and other learning events where you meet others.

Again, plan your networking events out over a year so you can budget for them. Seek out networking groups, coaches and mentors that will consistently challenge you to take your business to the next level. Periodically rehearse the message you want to convey. Be knowledgeable of the event and work the room. Know the questions to ask. Determine how you will follow up with your new contacts. Then, make an assessment for each event that you attend to determine which ones most met your expectations.

NETWORKING COMPONENT #7

PRESENCE

Ah, that magical first impression!

Rarely do you have more than ONE shot at making a dynamite first impression when networking with others! Even if people recognize you by your photograph on your website, have spoken with you on the telephone, or attended an event where you were the speaker ... meeting you one-on-one in conversation is a whole other matter!

You want to have that insatiable appetite for doing and saying things that place you at the center of things without overwhelming or monopolizing the conversation. You want to light a fire under the people you meet and openly stimulate their senses with genuineness and inspiration while learning as much as you can about them first before you talk about yourself. How do you do this? Let's get into that and how networking can and should become a way of life for you.

It's All In The Way You Present Yourself!

From the moment you get out of your car, or walk through the doors of the event room to the moment you say, "Good night, I enjoyed meeting you ... I'll call you tomorrow!" You should see yourself as a celebrity, an important person. Your degree of acceptance and interaction you experience will depend on how you identifiable you are.

People like people they can relate to. How you look, what you say, your body language such as how you hold your hands, your posture, manners, etc. can make all the difference when others for the very first time and every occasion.

This is one time when your image and what you say have a tremendous influence on whether people will do business with you! Sometimes, what people say about you AFTER you have departed a networking event means MORE to your success than what they say publicly. Feedback from others will become even more reinforcing if you have made that worthy first impression.

Factors that influence this initial impact are your handshake (firm, strong, dry not damp), facial expressions (smiling, sincere), eye contact (dead on, eye-to-eye), genuine interest in the success of others, and your overall attentiveness (engaged and on top of things).

Listen carefully for the person's name. If you don't hear or fully grasp a person's name, ask them to repeat it. If it's an unusual name, you may ask them to spell it for you to send the message that you want to be sure to pronounce it properly when referring him/her to your clients, for example. YOU can set the tone for a networking event by speaking with clarity and audible enough to be heard by your audience; not necessarily every person in the room. An easy thing to say, if unsure about what you heard, might be to say, "I'm sorry, can you repeat that? It's so loud in here, and what you said sounds very interesting!"

Make a powerful impression by putting others first before you tell your story. Find one thing you can comment on and ask them to expand on a topic a little with a couple more details. Be cautious that you aren't opening the door for a soliloquy. While you're not necessarily asking them to tell you the story of their life, you are intersted in ascertaining whether this person would be a valued contact for you to continue the conversation with at a later time after the event.

In most cases, demonstrating interest in others is a two-way street. It prompts the individual(s) to listen to you. Many people have experienced the person who may be speaking to you but his/her eyes are checking out the room in search of the next contact. Don't waste your time! Ask for a business cards, which will distract the person from sizing up new prey and move on.

Your objective is to **make a few new *quality contacts* at each networking meeting** and NOT to see how many cards you can acquire. The quality of the connection and the people you meet will become much more trusting of you if you concentrate on them.

Your posture and body language should be a show of confidence. Stand/sit up straight and leave a positive visual impression. Remember, there are no second chances when it comes to making a lasting first impression.

The clothing you wear reflects the type of person you are. Find out what the dress code is for the networking event you plan to attend: professional or business casual. Clothing should add value to your appearance and not detract from your persona. Wearing business attire assures that you are mature, professional, a member of the business community and take it seriously. This applies to men and women. Wear something that you believe you look good in. If you look good, you feel good.

Be comfortable but don't push the envelope with sandals or Levis. Take the dress code for the event account and put some thought into what you will wear. Business casual may mean different things to different companies. The key is to maintain a professional presence, even if you're not in a suit or tie. This is not the time to be a trailblazer or make a fashion statement.

Dress is not just about acquiring respect, but conveying it. Your appearance at a networking event is a mirror that reflects how you will be perceived. Try to fit into the business culture that you represent by showing some concern about the kind of image you and your company presents. Your appearance says a great deal about how you operate. Successful people tend to look the part.

Maintain healthy habits. Are you taking good care of yourself with a healthy diet and exercise? How you take care of you often translates to how much you care about your business and how you present yourself. If you find that you just don't have time to make healthy choices or even moderate exercise, the only person that will believe your excuses is YOU.

NETWORKING COMPONENT #8

CONVERSATION

WHAT should You say?

WHAT should You NOT say?

HOW should You say it?

WHEN should You say it?

WHO should You say it to?

Before we get too deep into this section, let's reflect back on the definition of "strangers?" Remind yourself, who the strangers represent when attending a networking function especially if you have reservations about introducing yourself to others:

> **"I no longer think of people as 'strangers.' Instead, we are all related and share similar needs in business and in life. Everyone in this room has a common goal -- to meet someone who can help them with their business ventures. I am one of those people. So, all we have to do is talk, listen, and enjoy the experience. Together, we have opportunities to connect and make networking really work! Hello, my name is _____."** How simple is that?

Most people begin forming an opinion of you within 3 seconds and these judgments can be difficult to change. Many of these "strangers" have the potential to become new friends, clients, affiliates, business contacts, service providers, and joint venture partners! Don't let these people go without at least talking to them first!

Your introduction should tell people who you are and it should encourage people to be interested in what you can contribute to a conversation. You need to sell yourself and feel confident while doing so because this will put others at ease.

All you have to do is talk to them. Easier said than done, right? Here are a number of great opening statements you can use to help break the ice, when networking for the first time. Let's start with how to introduce YOURSELF!

"Introductions" Made Simple!

When it comes to introducing yourself, follow these simple, but tried and true methods to break the ice and encourage a positive, informative dialogue. Also, be aware that as our business communities become more and more diversified, every culture has its own way of greeting people in business situations for the first time. Here are a few tips:

1. Take the initiative to make the first gesture to welcome someone to the event. It puts the other person at ease and opens the door to kick-start any conversation off right! If you make the first move and start asking questions, you get to kickback, so to speak, and LISTEN! Listening starts you off on the right track with building rapport while the other person gets to unload all about them. Another benefit to this tactic is you get to filter this person out. Do you want to learn more? Work with them? Move on? If you did all the talking up front, you'd never learn which move is best for you.

2. State your name and immediatly ASK A FEW QUESTIONS! Again, this gets the other person talking about themselves FIRST! *"Hi, my name's _____. What's yours? What do you do? How'd you hear about tonight's event?"* Practice making introductions until making introductions and asking questions flows more naturally for you. Most people enjoy talking about themselves so get them started down that road.

3. Now, only after hearing their story, consider (a) asking another question to show interest or (b) reply with your own short-story about what you do by pointing out something in common, or (c) if you don't think this person can add value to your business, ask for a business card because you never know who you are going to meet as you move on. By connecting individuals who may benefit from knowing each other without an immediate benefit to you is probably the icing on the cake for making yourself memorable. While networking, if you can focus on how you can help other people achieve their goals, then you have mastered the art of being there for others. Be a source for resources. Remember that it only takes a minute to make a strategic introduction that could prove invaluable to you indirectly and more directly to others. Take the time to make those connections and build on them. Always be of value to others and not just what you can take away from someone or the event.

4. Be a connector. People automatically look to these people when they need help meeting new people. Volunteer to introduce people to people. You also will have the option to launch into a brief presentation about what you do, but keep it short and sweet. We're filtering, remember? You'll later find out in this section why I take this approach. The quicker you can size up the other person, and wrap up your conversation, the sooner you can politely end the conversation and move on to someone else in the room. Time is short, and you don't have much of it when there are many great people to meet. Save the long version of what you do for a phone conversation or an appointment at a place of business. Networking is not about making 20 minute presentations. It's making an opening statement.

> **"Hello, what's your name? Tell me about yourself! ... Your business sounds interesting. Do you have a card or samples on you? Is it okay to call you this week? What day/time is best? ... Great! I look forward to talking to you some more! Let's move around the room and meet some more people, shall we?"** ~ YOU

5. Once you've both shared your contact information, quickly assess what your needs are regarding your new contact. Feel free to share any product literature, brochures, flyers, etc., but save your contact details for more viable prospects.

Manage your time well, because there are so many people to meet at that event that could turn into new leads, resources, customers, etc. Since you already know all about you, why not spend your time learning who's there, what they do and if you can help them by asking them what their needs are? There's a simple 80/20 rule you can follow that says LISTEN 80% of the time and SPEAK 20%. This rule could be advantageous in many conversations, both business or personal.

How do you keep the conversation going?

To keep any conversation moving along, here are a few suggested questions to ask to help make fact-finding fun while keeping the spotlight on the other person while you listen:

- **"So, what do you do?"**
- **"Where are you from?"**
- **"How did you get started (doing what you do)?"**
- **"How long have you been doing (that)?**
- **"What did you do before you _____?"**
- **"What's your background, experience, education?"**
- **"How did you hear about tonight's event?"**
- **"What made you decide to come to this event?"**
- **"What would you say you need the most help with?"**
- **"Do you know anyone here tonight?"**
- **"Have you met anyone tonight that can help you, ... impressed you? What do you think about the event?"**
- **"Do you have a website? How can I find out more about you?"**

You can just imagine how easy you can keep the conversation flowing in your direction by asking questions like the ones your just read, right? Since time is valuable, we all want to answer these two key questions sooner than later:

1. **CAN I HELP (THIS PERSON)?** *Directly* = Yes, you can help this person yourself with what you do/know/offer. *Indirectly* = no you can't help them directly, but maybe you can refer them to someone who can. Take their contact information and tell them you'll keep your ears/eyes open for someone who can help them as you walk around the room or leave to go back home or to the office.

2. **CAN (THIS PERSON) HELP ME?** Yes? Great! Exchange contact information and tell them you'll contact them this week to schedule a followup phone call to continue your conversation. No, they can't help you directly? Not to worry. Say, "thank you" and ask them to keep you in mind if they run across someone or a company who can. Next!

What TO say, what NOT to say, and definitely HOW to say it!

If you don't know how best to represent yourself, who will? How will you expect others to make a connection with you if you aren't clear about what it is you do, have to offer and how you can help people? WHAT you say to others and HOW you say it, how you ASK QUESTIONS, how you DON'T ask questions, WHEN to speak up, and, when NOT to speak (up) will have a direct impact on your networking success, believe me. For example, too much enthusiasm, fire-hosing people with all you've got to say about what it is you do, story-telling people to death without taking a breath on your part, interrupting too much, etc., will surely get you fired instantly as a potential anything in the eyes of the other person you're talking to when it comes to you making the most out of your time at the event.

• **When starting any conversation, ASK QUESTIONS.** Introduce yourself, sure. Say what you do if you have to, but turn the conversation around to the other person by asking questions. By listening first, you get more information to use when it's your turn to speak and the other person feels compelled to listen since you were so generous with your ears earlier. By listening more upfront, you can comment or reply more in detail to what the other person was saying to you. This goes a long way fast towards builds instant rapport. Now, if the other person beats you to the initial introduction, then respond with the appropriate response, but then quickly turn the conversation back around to the person.

• **Don't talk about yourself too much.** To generate even more interest in what you say, disclose just enough information to pique their interest and prompt questions. Give people more reasons to talk to you by NOT telling them so much about yourself. Maintain an element of mystery about you to some degree. Answer their questions directly. Don't hesitate to tell about your experiences and successes, but be obscure to incite feedback and contributions. Cultivate a conversation style of your own. I have and it works wonders. Alas, I wrote a few networking books about it! If people want to know about you, they'll ask. If they don't, you don't mind. You're fishing for people you can help. What's more, people naturally gravitate to others in the room who exude a relaxed, calm, caring, and knowledgable attitude with a little swag, a bit of savvy charisma and the humble presumption of success. Can you be or model all those? Absolutely!

• **Don't go on and on and brag about all your accomplishments.** Mention a few, but beyond that, who cares? Don't one-up anyone in a conversation, such as, "I just bought the newest model of whatever …" What value does that add to building rapport? People make statements like this because they crave attention. Not you. There's no problem with mentioning a particular success you had, if it helped others, but do so with the intent to share only if it might help the person in front of you or someone they might know. Also, *look-at-me* statements, such as, "I sold a billion books in one hour with the click of a button," can be more of a turn-off than turn-on. UNLESS, you can show others how to do it too.

Here's the rule, if YOU have to toot your own horn, chances are, there's probably not much there to toot about. Your ACTIONS and ACCOMPLISHMENTS should speak for you — not your WORDS. Let others find out or stumble upon these facts on their own. When OTHERS boast on your behalf, it's because they respect your accomplishments — they've experienced what you've been through, and are naturally inclined to tell others about YOU! They share in your success! *"So-and-so is so humble, you have no idea how much he can help you. He's just holding back some. Go ahead, ask him a question and see what his response is."*

How do you become "EXTRA-*ordinary?*" You do EXTRA-*things* that are out of the ordinary like working harder, faster, longer than the average person out there. When others speak about you, it's credible and more meaningful to others, because you naturally stood out among the crowd. Anytime you have that kind of community support, you should reciprocate by doing the same to others. What comes around, goes around, remember?

So, keep in mind, always: *Don't talk about yourself!* Let others do that for you. Actions (your deeds/accomplishments) speak louder than words.

• **Don't ask another question, or start another story especially if you want to leave the conversation.** You can get stuck in a group of semi-interested listeners if you're doing all the talking. Some people hesitate to move on for fear of insulting the person doing all the talking. Quickly assess whether what you are saying is of any value to those listening; otherwise, *zip de lip and* do everyone a favor and wrap it up. *"I could go on, but I'll stop here and take a breath. Besides, I want to meet some of the other people here tonight. That sound good?"*

• **Don't talk too loud, too fast, invade someone's space, or get in someone's face (too closely).** Keep your distance. Respect people's space and speak slowly so people understand you. Your tone should be at a comfortable listening level; clear and inviting to listen to. Even in a large crowd, there's no point in shouting because no one is listening. At least move off to the side and try again. Be conscious of how you sound when you talk. If you want feedback, ask someone you trust. You might get a good tip to slow down, speed up, pause more for feedback or speak up to be heard. If someone else is talking quickly, you can slow the pace by how you respond back to that individual ... talking slowly so they mirror your verbal responses. Try it. I've made it work. Subconsciously, you're setting the tone of the conversation. A good thing, for sure!

• **Talk in sound bites or in chunks of words, rather than an ever-lasting flow of words people can understand and remember!** If you happen to have a few popular sound bites or catch phrases you like to use in your pitch regarding your company/products/services, use them. If they are catchy and easy to recite, people will remember and associate them with you. A typical sound bite should sound like this: *"You have to tell it to sell it!"* Or, *"If we spend money on marketing, we have a problem!"*

If you get the chance, listen to the news, TV, radio and pick up a few good presentation tips. Listen to how the hosts go about discussing topics and talking to guests. You might also practice speaking in *interview-style sound bites* that relate to what you do and use them consistently so others associate them with you. It's one way to leave a memorable impression. By this I mean, don't talk on and on. Break up your presentation into specific points and pause for the other person to get a word in edgewise.

• **Don't interrupt others when they're speaking to you or others.** Wait for an opening in the conversation. Interrupt only if you have to move on or you have to leave the event. If you must interject a statement, apologize and say what you need to say.

• **Let people finish their own statements without YOU finishing them.** This is one of the most annoying misbehaviors in conversation. As much as you'd like to finish someone's statement or you know the answer to a question or you want to join in on the answer — DON'T! Allow the other person to complete their thought or sentence 100%. Practice restraint and wait your turn. When you show consideration, you should be able to expect the same respect in return. The problem with interruptions is the listening stops and the focus moves away from the speaker. The person that consistently interrupts is more focused on what he or she has to say. Unless you both see it coming and it's in the name of fun and laughter, that you both might appropriately say at the same time, "_____!"

Remember, talk less; let others talk more. There are some people who think that everything they have to say is fascinating and they never shut up. To be a highly effective conversationalist, there must be a balance between give and take. One way to discourage a big talkers is to ask if you have their permission to interrupt them when you have a thought or idea that relates to what they are saying.

This being the case, you have their permission to infuse a statement or two and eventually, you have created a dialogue. If this doesn't work, then you might be blunt about it and just say, *"Hey, can you let me get a word in edgewise? Otherwise, I'm going to forget my responses to the last 5-10 topics you brought up. I didn't want to be rude and interrupt, but allow me to comment on each thing you bring up. I'm fascinated by our discussion and I want in on it!"*

Channeling Conversation

Channeling means to listen intently to the other person while picking up cues, clues and body language in order to reflect the same "language" patterns (both verbal and physical) back to the other person for maximum communicational interaction. For example:

PERSON #1 — *"I'm interested* in learning more about what you do, your products/services. Can you tell me about them?"

PERSON #2 — "Absolutely, *I'm glad* to tell you about them. Which one are you most interested in?"

Channeling what someone else says requires that you listen intently and pick up on <u>keywords</u> that you can repeat back to them. This establishes an element of immediate familiarity for you and the other person most times without them realizing it. It's very effective. It also proves that you have been actively listening to what the other person said! Channeling takes practice. So, practice often by *networking often!!!*

Courteous Conversation

"Pardon me, do you have a minute?"

"Hi, am I calling at a good time?"

Whether networking in person or on the telephone, be respectful of other people's time. A person might be heading out the door, on their way to meet someone who just walked in, or they're just not available at the time you contacted them. Always ask if you are calling at a good time to talk. If the person you called does not have time, ask for a more convenient time to contact him/her. They'll appreciate the fact that you cared to respect their time. MOST people call and just talking your ear off with no respect to what you might be doing in that given moment. Don't YOU be like that.

Upon closing any conversation, in which you were on the receiving end for help, reciprocate and ask if there's anything you can do to assist the person who helped you? Everyone's time is valuable. Respect theirs. If you did call for help, don't abuse it and call them daily, weekly, all the time without offering to help them in some way (i.e., paying for their time, buying them lunch, offering up your time in some way to help them, etc.).

When you talk to people face-to-face or on by phone, put their needs **FIRST**!

Whether you call someone or personally meet that individual, don't start talking about what YOU want/need right away. Here are some great starter questions to kick off the perfect phone conversation:

- **"Pardon the interruption, but do you have a minute?"**
- **"Am I calling at a good time?"**
- **"Is this a good time for me to introduce myself?"**
- **"What's new and exciting in your business now?"**
- **"Do you have time to hear a great idea?"**

- **"Can you advise me on _____?"**
- **"How's your family (e.g., name them if can)?"**
- **"What are your thoughts on _____?"**
- **"Can you share what's working for you in _____?"**
- **"How's your day going? Can I do anything to help?**

Bottom line, always, be respectful of other people's time. They might be having a bad day or they're under some kind of pressure that you don't know about. Maybe your call MAKES their day or it's an interruption. Another great idea is to text them, "Free to talk?" Then, they can reply with *"Yes, call ..."* or *"Give me 10 minutes ..."*

Again, don't just start off with business. Ask about them personally. How are they doing? Show you care about them as a "human being" and just not some answer/resource vending maching you go to when you're hungry. Listen, sincerely AND closely! By LISTENING FIRST to them, you'll pick up clues as to how they're feeling (in the moment) and if NOW really IS a good time to talk. This also works well when you meet people at networking events. For example ...

- **"Hi, (their name), do you have a minute?"**
- **"How do you like the event so far?"**
- **"Any good leads, yet?"** *(Small talk; opens people up to talk to you.)*

Show a genuine interest in what they have to say and how they say it. If it sounds like they're having a bad day/night, you might ask, "Are you okay?"; or "Is everything alright?", and stay off the business topics until you're sure they're okay. They might not be feeling very well, and it would help them a lot if you could either hear their story or (perhaps) call the event planner over to help them or just lend a sympathetic ear to what's ailing them. Maybe they've had a bad networking night and you're the person who could help them. You just made a new friend, and maybe a new customer! If things are okay, and they're just catching their breath, then casually proceed to discuss what's on your mind:

- "The reason I called was ..."

- "The reason I walked over here ..."

- "The reason I came tonight was ..."

- "I wanted to ask you about ..."

- "Would you be interested in ..."

And, ask nicely! People love to help other people when they know they're truly appreciated at the other end. No one wants to be at the beck and call anyone.

When you call people on the phone, or meet them in person, have something "positive" to say to them before you get started with the intended business.

Again, just don't call people up and start talking business.

"Yes, can you ... (do what I need right now) ..."

Instead, when you call people, show respect for interrupting their busy day or relaxing evening ...

"Yes, hey, how are you doing? Yeah? What's new and exciting? Yeah? Really ... And, ...? Well, the reason why I called was ..."

In this way, you make a personal connection first. You gave them a break from their tired day to talk about something fun. Having been refreshed, they'll be all ears to listen to you and why you called. Chances are, they're more apt to jump right on what you need than if you had tried the "Hello, I'm calling because I need you to ... and will you do this for me? Thanks!" Remember, you get more with honey, than you do with vinegar, every time. Other ways to introduce the conversation is to:

(1) **Give the other person an idea** that might help their business, before you get into your needs.

(2) **Give them a new lead or contact for their business** before you present your circumstances and what you would like to ask of that person.

(3) **Always make an effort to reciprocate!** If you are asking for a particular lead and you are successful getting the referral, ask if there is any way you can assist them. You'd be surprised how they'll respond. For example:

> **(YOU) "Sure, let me run this past you — we're launching a new ad campaign, and I'd like your opinion." (OTHER PERSON) "Sure thing, I'm all ears!"**

Then, the two of you are working together to help solve each other's needs. Remember the "art of giving?" When you give, you receive! So, if you want something from someone, you should offer to give something to them first. I always do, and it pays off every time!

This goes the same for "over delivering!" If you ask someone to do something for you, and in turn, you promise to do something for them, "over deliver" what you promised you would do. That pays off in the long run too! Doing more for others helps them do more for you when you least expect them too. A nice thing, for sure.

Remembering Names

Remembering names is a real challenge for some people, especially when networking. Today, more than ever, we're exposed to so many people online and offline. How can you be expected to remember everyone's name? We've all experienced this dilemma at one time or another, right? You could, of course, apologize for your shortcoming and ask the person to tell his/her name again. It's honest and understandable. BUT, you're not going to do that, unless it's absolutely necessary. On the other hand, when you call someone by name, they are flattered that you remember who they are. So, let's talk about remembering names, shall we?

There are simply two main reasons why we forget people's names:

1. You've never heard their name <u>BEFORE</u>. The name is new to you and not in your memory bank. What we don't have, we can't recall. How many of you know the name of the clerk you see all the time at your local grocery store? How about the mailman you chat with daily or the mechanic who fixed your car last month? Maybe you don't know their names because you never asked or even checked their name tag.

2. You haven't heard their names <u>ENOUGH TIMES</u>. Their name hasn't been repeated enough times for our brains to readily feed their name right back to you. How many of you know your mother's maiden name or your father's middle name? How about your sibling, classmate, co-worker, or business associate? Exactly.

Well, there are several techniques for remembering names and here are just a few that really work:

The "Echo Effect," as I call it.

Often, when you're introduced to someone, your attention is not on their name but what they're saying. You may be thinking about other things such as how to shake hands, what to say, maybe they said their name too fast, so you missed hearing their name and now you are too embarrassed to ask for it. Well, here's one of my favorite ways to remember names, and it works every time. I call it *"The Echo Effect."*

Earlier in **My Networking Tactics**, we spoke about the procedures for meeting someone for the first time.

#1 YOU: When shaking hands say, "Hi, how are you, my name is (____), **what's your name?**"

#2 OTHER: "My name's **Jade**, nice meeting you."

#3 YOU: "Hi **Jade**, I'm glad to meet you. Tell me about yourself ..." (Get them to start talk about themselves first, remember?)

Now, while they're talking to you about themselves, here's your chance to exercise *"The Echo Effect"* to remember their name. Upon hearing their name once, make a conscious, yet silent, effort to repeat their name to yourself (mentally) at least 5-10 times or more and then use their name again when speaking to them.

#1 YOU: "Hi, how are you, my name is (____), what's your name?" *(e.g., when shaking hands)*

#2 THEM: "My name's **Jade**, great to meet you ..."

#3 YOU: "Hey Jade, tell me about yourself .... *(While the other person is talking, you mentally repeat their name in your head like an "ECHO" ... "Jade, Jade, Jade, Jade, Jade, Jade ...")*

How long does it take you to recite a name 5-10 times in your head to get the name seeded in your memory bank so you can recall it later with ease? Seconds. It's an easy trick to learn.

I'll give you a great example of where I used this technique, which I coined, *"The Echo Effect."* I was attending the birthday party for the daughter of a friend. We were all told to meet at a specific restaurant. Upon arrival, we were seated at a large table that sat about 20 people. As people were seated, we went around the table introducing ourselves to everyone while sharing how we each knew the birthday girl. As people announced their name, one at a time, I began to "echo" or "recite" their names in my mind for the duration of their introductions.

John, John, John, John, John, ...

Mark, Mark, Mark, Mark, Mark, Mark, ...

Vivienne, Vivienne, Vivienne, Vivienne, ...

Sue, Sue, Sue, Sue, Sue, Sue, ...

Bob, Bob, Bob, Bob, Bob, Bob, ...

Dominique, Dominique, Dominique, ...

Mary, Mary, Mary, Mary, Mary, ...

... YOU GET THE IDEA ...

After everyone finished sharing their name and story, a few people walked in late and missed all of the formal introductions. I volunteered to introduce everyone at the table. I was then asked to introduce John, Mark, Vivienne, Sue, Bob, Dominique, etc.

To many people's surprise, I astonished them by remembering 12+ names. *"The Echo Effect"* worked. They were also aware that I hadn't previously met anyone except the immediate family so there was no way I could have made those introductions without this technique.

"The Echo Effect" works well in a group setting or single setting if you aren't particularly good with names. When it comes time to use someone's name again in conversation, you can recall it quickly and easily, because you repeated it over and over again in your head.

"**Wow, that's great, Jade. You and I have a lot in common. Do you have a card, Jade? Let's talk more about this sometime this week, shall we? Great, thanks, Jade.**"

Write Their Name Down

Sometimes it helps to write down the names of people we meet with a little information about what you talked about. You might do this right after you speak with them.

This is especially helpful in a group setting where a number of people are gathered and each person calls out their name. As they do this, make a list of names on a piece of paper in the order they call out their name and say what they do. You might also draw a circle or rectangle of the table like a seating chart to help you remember who they are because you can visualize where they sat. Then, throughout the meeting, review your chart for who's who when they are speaking. When it comes time to meet and greet, you already know their names, because you wrote them down.

It also might help to associate a name with something you will remember about that person, something that makes sense maybe only to you. Perhaps, something their wearing, a question they asked you, etc., will identify that person to you.

Write notes on the business cards you receive from the people you meet to capture a comment or suggestion or characteristic or the topic you discussed.

Suppose you remember a person's first name, but forget their last name? Don't worry. You'll find out later when you get their business card. Or, often times, the only time you really need their last name is when you're writing them a check (and you need their full name); go ahead and ask for the spelling of both (and you'll get the latter). Or, if they're signing up to be an affiliate for you or buying something from you, then they'll be filling in a form with their full name anyway. Then, there you'll have it, both their first and their last name.

Ask For Their Website

Ask for his/her website address. Every now and then, you'll find the website address includes the person's name in it:

GaylMurphy.com, JohnSantangelo.com, DrAndreaPurcell.com, etc.

When you discover that the domain names (a.k.a., website address) have their name in it, you can probably call them by their first name.

YOU: "Do you have a website?"

OTHER: "Yes, it's JohnSantangelo.com."

YOU: "Great, John, can you tell me more about what you do? Your business sounds very interesting."

See how easy that is? Yeah ...

Introduce The Person To Others

Using someone's name repeatedly can help you remember their name, too.

"Alan, I'd like you to meet Bill, Jim-Bob and Betty-Lee. Everyone, please meet Alan, he's from ..."

Keep A Mental Image Of Someone's Individual Nametag

If you are a visual person, you might be able to remember what their nametag said if you take a firm mental picture of it in the beginning and then glance to it from time to time. during the conversation. I've done this before. Where you look long at their nametag when you first meet them, or when they're talking to you. Recalling this picture helps to recall the name as well.

Other Tips For Remembering Names

If you forgot a name, don't worry. The other person, whose name you forgot, will no doubt contact you. When they do, they'll reintroduce themselves.

"Hey Bart, it's BETTY. We met at the networking event last night. You may recall that I was interested in your video tutorials and your new book."

See what they just did? She just gave you her name and I remember her well because she said she'd call me about tutorials and my book.

Ask For Correct Spelling

Another way to learn a person's name is to **ask for the spelling of it** because you want to add it to your list, correctly. He/she will be pleased that you asked unless the last name is "Smith." This works when you're autographing a book they just bought from you, or you want to write their name and telephone number down. Just ask, "How do you spell your name?" If they say, "Sue" or "Sam" or "Tom" or "Joe" or "Mary" or "Tim" ... you can laugh and say, "I know, but some people have different ways of spelling a name and I just wanted to make sure I spelled yours correctly. Thanks."

You can also **find out what their name is from an order form or a mailing list** you ask them to fill out. Thank them for completing it, review the name (spelling), etc. and reply, "Thanks, Karen."

Fake It Until You Make It.

Sometimes, you just have to **fake it until you make it**. Whatever you do, avoid the embarrassing mistake of asking, "What was your name again?" Try exercising one of the previous tips on remembering names before you are forced to admit, "I'm sorry that I forgot your name. Please tell me again?"

Let their name come to you. Conceal the fact you don't know it by listening to others recite it. You can also let it surface in other ways. For example, a person might repeat his/her name to someone else within the group you are in. There you go. You just go their name again.

When all else fails and you absolutely can't recall someone's name, face it. Anyone can forget a name. Just be honest about it and then admit you have forgotten it. People understand and they are accommodating.

Other Ways To Remember Names

There are other techniques for remembering people's names and here are a few of those examples.

• **Associate a name to a common word you will remember.** For example, the last name Chandelier might sound like "channel deer" or "Ted" like "Lead" ... Try it out. It this technique for you, great. Still, repeat the person's name in your mind over and over again, 5-10 times until you get it. Or, just look at their name tag or business card if they have one. Duh.

• **Associate the person's name with someone you already know.** The new name is Bob. Think of your Uncle Bob. Just be careful you don't call him Uncle Bob. Great, now you've got a number of Uncle Bob, and Aunt Grace and President George catalogued in your brain. What happens when you meet another Bob, Grace or George? This is might not be *the* best technique to use, but people do use it. Again, the easier way to remember a name is by reciting it silently about 5-10 times in a row as soon as you hear the name.

Conversational "Opening Questions"

Here are three questions for networking conversations that go beyond the obvious question ... *"What do you do for a living?"*

1. **YOU: "Hi, tell me about yourself ..."** This is an easy question to start people off talking about themselves, and, by default, they'll probably tell you what they do too without you asking that question. While they talk, repeat their name to yourself 5-10 times so you remember it.

2. **YOU: "What do you like most about what you do?** *or* **What got you into doing what you're doing?** *or* **What's your background/education/training to do that?"** Get the other person revved up about what they do by asking them what is it they like most about doing what they do or how they got started. As they talk, you're listening and learning. What are they saying? Are they giving away any clues as to who their ideal client is or how you might be able to help them?"

3. **YOU: "What kind of help do you need most in your business?** *or* **How can I help you?"** These are powerful questions to ask at this juncture. After hearing about the other person, why they do what they do, how they got started, what they love about doing what they do, you can now ask what kind of help do they need. Watch them open up to you with either something specific or something general and naturally anticipated. "You can help me find clients." "You can become a client, affiliate, ..." "I'm looking for ..." You just never know what you can do for people. These three questions get everyone you talk to off on the right foot in your direction: 1) talking about themselves, 2) you listening for ways to respond with surgical precision, and 3) if you can help them, directory or indirectly, how.

Topics To Avoid In Conversation

Some say there are certain topics you should probably avoid when striking up conversation, that is, unless it is a topic for your meeting or networking event, or you're very knowledgeable about the subject. Topics such as **politics**, **war**, **religion**, **money**, **health** and even **relationships** don't always make great conversation *starters*.

Sometimes, and without knowing on your part, these topics can be awkward when speaking with people you just met. If the subject comes up, I'd recommend you let the other person do *most* of the talking and reply with generalized, unbiased comments, largely because you don't know the other person's opinions and beliefs. Let alone, you don't want to be roped into a conversation destined to taking up more time than you'd probably prefer. Remember, you've got people to meet, not listen to their soap box discussion about whatever's upsetting them about whatever in the moment. Move on.

If you *are* pushed for a response, and if you're uncomfortable giving one, you could simply say, *"You know, that's a pretty interesting topic, and I don't know if we have time to talk about those matters here, only because, I'm more interested in meeting as many people as I can, and in the interest of time, let's table that topic for another meeting. Sound good? BYE."*

Conversation Topics You Could Discuss & Focus On While You're Networking

1. **Allow the other person to talk about their successes and concerns for their business**, while you listen intently. Gathering this kind of kind of information can help you map out solutions to their problems and offering ideas on how your company could service their business. Get to know as many people as possible. Listen to their stories and speak briefly of your own.

2. **Ask the host to introduce you to a few people** and say a few things others might be interested in knowing. Ensure that the host introduces you per your specific information needs. It can be advantageous to provide the host with a short script and have them read it word-for-word.

3. **Give real praise to help raise the self-esteem** of others, especially when you can see the need for it.

4. **Keep the conversation business-related and never personal.** Leave your personal stories at home. Stick to business. Your private life is just that, private.

5. **While the other person is talking to you or introducing you,** you can contemplate on what you are hearing.

6. **By listening, you pick up on "hot buttons,"** which makes it easier for you to spin the conversation right back at them with your input or more questions.

7. **Find one positive/attractive/great thing about the other person** and share it with him/her. It will boost confidence and leave a positive, long-lasting impression in that person's mind about you.

8. **Offer ideas and solutions** to help others with their business by listening to them first.

9. **Make opportunities to follow up** with business acquaintances. Keep your conversations short, for networking purposes, but let them know, you'd like to continue your conversation later, on the phone or over lunch. Suggest, "There are a lot of people here for us to meet tonight. I can tell you are as eager as I am to get started. Would Thursday at 12:00 P.M. work for you? How about meet at your office or talking over lunch?"

You can imagine these techniques really helping you to advance your networking agenda for success.

Speaking Without Interrupting

I mentioned this earlier, but it's worth repeating. Sometimes, *enthusiasm* can be misinterpreted. Show interest, yes, but don't be too eager to tell your WHOLE story in 10 minutes or less without allowing others to get their thoughts and ideas across too. Too much *enthusiasm* (or nervous energy) might prevent you from letting others finish their statements. If you sense you're in a hurry to contribute to the conversation, hold your horses, and wait your turn. It's better that way. Don't interrupt or try to speak for someone, either. Keep it professional, always. Others will notice that great conversational quality about you ... courtesy and more.

Telephone Conversations

- **When you say you will call someone back — DO IT.** Don't make a commitment you can't follow through on.

- **Answer the phone promptly**, preferably within three to four rings. If you can't answer the phone, don't answer it just to tell someone, "I can't talk right now." Let voicemail tell them, or text them, "I'm in a meeting right now," or "I'm on a call. Will call you back."

- **Speak up. Speak clearly.** You want to come across well-spoken, clear-minded and understood.

- **If you're leaving a voice mail message, leave your phone number TWICE at the end.** State your business and when giving your number, repeat the number at the end of the message. It makes it easy for the person to write it down without having to replay the message.

- **Smile (or even stand up) when you are talking on the phone**. It manifests itself by your tone and gives a pleasant impression.

- **Add "Thank you for calling"** or "I look forward to _____" or "Let's talk again soon," at the end of calls. You might even try this formula for saying goodbye ... "Great, yes, we'll talk again soon ..."

- **When hanging up the phone, wait a few seconds before clicking the END CALL button.** It can be a tad offensive to hear someone hang up before you can utter your last word. Instead, wait three to five seconds, then hang up. You might also let the other person hang up first. I do that every now and then. The last thing they'll remember about a call from you is what you talked about and not that abrupt click/hang up you pulled on them. Show respect for their mind and memory and be aware of how you end your calls. It too could make a lasting impression.

Voice Mail Messages & Greetings

If you cannot get to the phone by the third ring, let it go to voice mail and then call the person back. Why? Suppose you are on another call. If you can't talk, don't put the caller on hold. Let voice mail handle talking to them. Even if you're about to wrap up a call, let the incoming call go to voice mail. Don't interrupt your current conversation by asking to put that person on hold only for a few minutes, while you tell someone you can't talk right now. That is, unless, it's a family member or emergency and you have to take that call. After all, you can call the second caller right back within a few seconds. Allow additional calls to go to voice mail when you're on the phone. Again, unless that incoming call is an emergency or a call you've been waiting for, explain this to your current caller and proceed to accept the incoming call. I usually text the person calling in, "I'm on the phone. Will call you right back. Thanks."

Another reason for letting calls go to voice mail is to see if what the caller's needs can be handled with a return phone call or an eMail. Time is money. If you answer the phone, you might get tied up for longer than you have time for compared to letting it go to voice mail. After listening to their voice mail message, you might have a quick solution to the request without engaging in some long conversation. You might even text or email them the answer to their request. Or, if you decide to call, "I just called to give you the answer you're looking." Do you need a simple, yet successful voice mail greeting script to record on your voice mail? Try this one on for size. I've used it for years and it works like a charm every time:

"Hi, this is _____. Thanks for calling. I'm sorry that I'm unable to take your call right now, but your call is important to me. So, please leave your name, your telephone number twice, and a brief message. I'll return your call as soon as I can. Again, thanks for calling."

Record this greeting with a calm and relaxed voice so your callers feel warm and welcomed to leave a message. Rehearse the script and record it until you're satisfied with your tone and delivery. I personally like reading from a script I typed into the computer so I know exactly what I'm saying and how I want to say it. If you read it a few times, it'll become familiar to you and it won't sound like you're actually reading text. OR, you might have someone else read your greeting message for you to give it an element of authority. "Thank you for calling the office of Bart Smith. He can't come to the phone right now, but your call is important to him. Please ..."

The Storyteller

Storytelling is one of the greatest networking skills you can possess when it comes to talking to others and getting others to believe in your message. Ultimately, they may hire you, buy product from you or promote your services to others. How do you become a great storyteller? Follow these very simple steps:

1. **By listening to other people tell stories and repeating the interesting ones to other people,** this will become one of the best ways to become a great story teller. Then practice, practice, practice.

2. **Another way to become a storyteller** is to use your own life experiences. Link lessons and messages in them to situations relating to your current audience, whether it's one person or one hundred.

3. **Practice telling all kinds of stories to other people**, no matter where you are, in business or casual environments.

4. **Each time you tell a special story about your life or business experience**, your script will improve. The more you tell your story, any story ... the better that story will sound when you tell it the next time and thereafter. Practice makes perfect.

5. **Telling personal stories** shows your humanity and helps to lower the anxiety level most people feel when attending

a meet and greet for the first time.

6. **Telling your story allows others to see what they have in common with you.** This is a subtle way to build rapport and commonality among others without having to say, "Will you be my friend?"

7. **Adding new stories from your life experiences**, talking to others, meeting new people, watching new television programs, reading new magazines, reading new websites and listening to audio are resources to enhance a story. The more stories and information you absorb, the more thoughts, ideas, facts, stories you'll have to turn into an unlimited number of features you can share with others.

Don't Sell, Instead, Story-TELL To Impress

It's never the right time or place to openly "sell" at a networking event. No one wants to be put on the spot to buy something. If you share what you know and motivate them enough about the benefits of your product, people may ask to purchase an item on the spot without exchanging any merchandise. In other words, they bought your delivery, your style, and have confidence in what you can offer them.

Then, after the meeting, you can direct interested buyers to your "buy me" link or sample, etc. While networking is the time and place to meet others, you can still hone your "presentation skills."

Learn how to present your products and services in such a way that people actually become INSPIRED to buy now.

Open-Ended Questions

When open-ended questions are asked, it encourages others to think through their responses. In this way, we learn more about what they know, think and feel. A "yes" or "no" response adds no value to a conversation. Examples of open-ended questions are:

- "What's your background?"

- "How did you get started in the business you're in?"

- "What made you want to write your book?"

- "How long did it take you to write your book and what inspired you to write it?"

- "What kind of services do you offer? How much?"

- "Who is your ideal client? Can I be one of them?"

- "What challenges does your company face when it comes to marketing and finding new clients?"

- "What's the best business advice anyone gave you?"

Avoid asking questions that will evoke a one-word response.

Small Talk

Small talk is great when you're waiting for an event to start or a friend to arrive. Small talk is the friendly art of talking to people about surface topics that don't go too deep into what you might really want to talk about, but you really don't have the time or it's not really the right place to have that conversation.

How can you make small talk work for you? Use it to learn the other person's name and use it in your conversation. Then, share your name and what you do. That's small talk.

Don't forget to add your website address into the conversation. Ask if they'd like more information about your products or services. Give them a flyer, postcard and/or business card.

Here's a tip that gets people's attention ... Let folks hold your book or other products while you are speaking to them. In a brief moment, you give someone a glimpse into your life through your products and what you have to say. To continue a conversation, suggest a time after the event, a phone call or a meeting to discuss your business with more details.

Joining & Leaving Groups

How do you leave an event without coming across as an intruder or a rude runaway? Follow these guidelines for conversation do's and don'ts.

Joining Groups ...

Listen to the topic being spoken about and then add a few nuggets of information for a solid contribution. Keep it short and allow others to take control of the conversation again. They'll ask you for more data provided your input added value.

Successfully joining a group is about timing, making a value-added contribution and sharing a platform with others. It requires focus on different viewpoints and respect for each speaker.

Leaving Groups ...

Depending on the nature of the group and its size, leaving might be easier than you think. It's best to give a legitimate reason for your departure and bow out gracefully.

Leaving Large Groups ...

You can always get up and walk away. You don't need make an excuse if you're with a group of strangers or in a group of five or more. Just quietly (and confidently) leave.

If you are sitting or standing next to someone and the two of you had only a brief conversation, you might say, "I'll be right back ..." Or, "I must leave. It was great meeting you."

Usually in large groups, someone else is doing the speaking and getting the attention. While the others are captivated by the speaker, you're free to depart.

If you're doing the speaking and you're in a large group, just wrap it up and say, "I have to make this short. If I didn't get someone's card, do make sure I get one and we'll talk soon." Or, "I regret that I have to run. It was a pleasure meeting all of you."

Leaving A Small Group or One Person ...

The smaller the group (five or less), the harder it is to leave because it becomes obvious that you are leaving even if it's for a very good reason.

> **"Hey, I have to run, but it was great meeting all of you. Let's stay in touch ... make sure I have your info."**
>
> **"Hey, (to one person in the group), I have your number, I'll call you. (To the others) ... It was nice meeting you. I have to scoot ..."**

Speaking to one person or everyone in a group, reassure people that you have their contact information and you'll reach out to them later. Tell them you enjoyed meeting them and look forward to more dialogue at a later date. Then, make good on your word.

There are many excuses you can give when you want to leave a conversation/group. Suggestions include making excuses to use the rest room, run to your car, check the parking meter, make a phone call, speak to someone who just walked in, catch someone before he/she leaves, buy something at the product table in the back of the room (or in the hallway) before closing, etc.

Or, offer that you are hungry and have to get something to eat or drink before you pass out, or you're exhausted and need to leave.

I'm sure you get the picture. Whatever you come up with, make your excuse believable so no one is offended by your leaving or misunderstands your motive.

Avoid The Following

Pressing someone for free advice is never a good idea, unless you do something for them in like return. This is not the time or place to press for *more* information. If you want advice, make an appointment to see that person at their office or speak with the person by phone. In both cases, schedule the time. If someone presses you for free advice, direct them to your website where they can opt-in to your newsletter, or ask them, "Do you want the 60 second answer, the 6-minute answer or the 60-minute answer?" No matter their response, yours would be, "Well, I have 60 seconds to tell you that it would take more than six minutes to do discuss (x-topic). What I really need is a full hour (60 minutes), and we can then talk about (x-topic) in detail. How's that sound, oh, and my fee is _____." You get the idea. Don't let people push you around asking YOU for free advice either.

Criticizing others either in person or after they've left a group is highly inappropriate even if everyone might agree with you. This is not professional behavior. If someone else has nothing good to say about another person, don't engage. Make your way out of that circle.

Talking too much. Remember the golden rule in conversation when networking: talking MORE is LESS EFFECTIVE and talking LESS is MORE effective. Carefully choose words to form statements and questions that will make the most impact. Be factual, interesting and stay focused on the prize — networking for solid contacts and referrals.

Talking too loud. When speaking to someone directly, that conversation is usually private and should be between the two of you. You don't always want other people listening in on your conversation. Keep the business you discuss between the person or group you're speaking with. Naturally, you want to be heard, and you think you will attract more attention if you turn your volume up a notch. This can be a good way to gain the right kind of attention, but it needs to be carefully orchestrated. Loud mouths are just plain annoying, so be aware of those you're with. Don't talk too loud.

Take It Slow & Easy

No one enjoys networking with people who talk too fast or push too hard for help or to make a sale. Like all relationships, business relationships take time to grow. Get to know people by first listening to them. Throughout the entire evening, look back on those you met, and ask yourself who would you really feel comfortable working with? Did someone give you a tip about who to work with and not to work with? This could be valuable information. Monitor how fast you talk and slow yourself down when you get excited. We've all been there; myself included.

Politely, Get Away From People Who Talk Your Ear Off

If you find yourself trapped in a conversation with a non-stop talker, and you know it's time to move on, here's what you can say (to them) to courteously make your departure.

"Hey (TALKER'S NAME), I don't mean to interrupt, but let's do this ... Give me your contact information, I'll give you mine (optional), and let's continue our conversation after the event tonight so we can meet some of the other people we haven't met here before they leave and the event is over." Then, jingle your car keys in your pocket. It'll psychologically trigger a "Oh, time to go ..." mental response and you can quickly put an end to that conversation.

Silence Is Golden

Did you know that the person who does the least amount of talking can actually control the conversation? Carefully adding short or long pauses between remarks can add emphasis to what you say. When it's your turn to talk, because you paused and were patient while the other person spoke, you can use the opportunity to make a comment about what was discussed, and also a closing statement to continue the conversation later and leave to meet others.

Impolite Talkers

If you find someone dominating your time, interrupting you, speaking loudly, cutting you off at every sentence, here are a few suggestions:

- **"HEY, we can't hear the speaker."** Then, give them a *LOOK.*

- **"I have a few more people I need to meet before they leave**. It was great meeting you. Can we talk later?"

- **"Let's agree to meet later** to finish this conversation."

- **"You know, *Mother Nature* is calling me**, and I have to run. Can we talk later? Thanks."

- **"Would you excuse me**, I need to check in with (person/ your car/parking meter, etc.)."

- **"Listen,** I need to meet a few more people who just arrived, but if you'll give me your business card, I'll know how to reach you when I need your services. Thanks."

Your "Elevator Pitch"

- **Know what you do** and how to say it in 30-60 seconds.

- **Write it down**, read it over and over; memorize it. Repeat it until it becomes natural. Shorten it if it's too long.

- **The same pitch won't fit all situations**, so create a variety of pitches based on your skill-set, service interests, types of clients you seek, etc. Again, write-memorize, read-rehearse it until it exudes confidence.

- **An elevator pitch is not a sales pitch**. It's informative and motivating, not pushy or cheesy.

- **Your elevator pitch isn't about you**, but what you do that helps others. Don't mention achievements or make boastful comments about your company. Identify what your company does and what you do for people. The people listening to you will be interested in what you can do for them. Keep your pitch focused on them only.

- **If they want to know your name**, they'll ask you. Your pitch doesn't have to include your name, but it can. "Hi, my name is ____, and I assist people with ____."

- **"Hurt and Rescue."** Your elevator speech should highlight problems people have and the solutions you can provide. It's what you do best. Stick to one problem/solution per pitch. Don't attempt to mix it up for different products/services. Create one pitch per product/service and deliver it to a specific/niche group/person.

- **Keep your pitch short** so people don't turn away or drop out. This isn't a presentation. It's a 20-second speech. Keep it short and simple. Leave time at the end for people to ask a couple of questions or make comments such as, "How do you do provide that service?" Or, "I know someone who can use your services. I can."

- **When speaking before a crowd of people, state your name**, "Hi, my name is ____." Then, you can add what you do and who you're looking to serve such as, "I do _____ and am looking for people who want or need ____."

- **Practice makes perfect.** The more you practice your pitch, the more comfortable you will be delivering it. Ask your friends and associates to hear it and give you feedback prior to any presentation. You're ready to network when you feel confident about your pitch.

- **Be yourself, be natural and be flexible**. Sometimes, you can be free to alter, modify or change your pitch on the spot when talking to others. Be flexible and spontaneous. Others will appreciate it.

Proper Introductions

When it comes to making introductions, keep them simple, professional and candid.

- **Introduce people who just approached or joined the group.** Make them feel welcome. Help break the ice for them.

- **Introduce people by their first name** and last name if you know it.

- **Introduce individuals to a group first** and vice versa, one person at a time, slowly and with clarity.

- **Introduce people with titles included in their name** such as Dr. Michael Smith, Sergeant John Smith, Sir K.K. Downing, etc.

- **Know the basic order for making introductions.** If you are making the introductions in a group, ideally introduce men to women first ("Susan, meet George"); a younger person to an older person ("Timmy, this is Mr. Rogers"); professional to a non-professional ("Betty-Lee Zorba, this is Dr. Rosen.") It shows respect.

- **Include the relationship people have to you in your introduction** ... "Hello, this is John, my business partner ..." Or, "Greetings. This is my good friend, _____." Or, "Hi, this is my mother, _____." If you're introducing a couple who is married, you might say, this is "Mr. and Mrs. _____." Or, if you're introducing two people who live together, just introduce them as "Ben and Cherri."

- **It's okay to use the phrase 'my wife' or 'my husband'** when introducing your spouse or partner.

- **If you forgot the name of someone who you'd like to introduce,** just apologize for not remembering their name, and make the introduction. "I'm sorry. I have forgotten your name. Everyone, this is _____."

- **If you're at an event and you know the host**, however the host neglects to introduce you to the other guests, feel free to introduce yourself. Make sure you mention how you know the host and why you're attending the event.

Mixed Messages

Be specific about who you are and what you do. People's time is valuable. In my book, *My TV/Radio Interview Tactics & Checklists*, I talk about how to perfect your pitch to whomever you talk to:

> "Today's most precious commodity is our 'attention span!' It's literally worth $millions if you can get your message in there amidst the colossal other marketing messages aimed at people every day!"

I've got a ton of info in this book about doing interviews, coming up with sound bites and much more. So, check it out at my website:

BartSmith.com/books

NETWORKING COMPONENT #9

ACTIONS

What Do You Do Before, During, & After Networking With People?

With all there is to know and learn about networking, I've broken some of it down into what you need to do **before, during and after** every networking event!

What To Do <u>BEFORE</u> The Networking Event

Prepare for your networking experience!

Make a checklist of things you want to take with you, share and do at the event. Be sure you have sample product/books, flyers, postcards, copies of press releases and more. Make sure your car is clean and you look sharp. Don't walk into the event having forgotten something! The media could be attending your event and without press releases, you miss a prime opportunity to get recognized.

Research Companies That Will Attend The Event, Especially The Company Hosting It

Check out the websites of people you plan to meet at the networking event, and the company that's hosting the networking event. Read up on who's associated with the company, what they do, a background on the company and take that information to the event. Have questions prepared. Being well-prepared before the event will help you fit in instantly!

Arrive with a mission and topics ready to discuss before you attend the event. Most of the people we randomly meet at networking get-togethers are not always in a position to buy your services or help you with your goals, so don't expect it. This takes some of the pressure off you to produce and sell. Use the time wisely to relax, mingle and get to know others.

What's most important will be for you to establish yourself in people's memory by making a good impression as someone that appears approachable and trustworthy and stay connected to you following the event.

Come EARLY ... Stay LATE!

Inexperienced networkers come to meetings late and leave as soon as the speaker has finished. The best opportunities for networking are before and after the program. Consequently, if you go only to listen to the speaker, you are missing out on the experience of networking and the priceless value and opportunities you could experience.

Arrive early, check in and tour the event facility. Observe people going into the meeting to familiarize yourself with them before the event starts. This pays big dividends later when you meet them for the first time. You already know them by sight. This can help to diffuse any anxiety about networking.

Arriving early allows you to check the place out, as well as the people. Enter the event room, even before it's set up. Observe people setting it up. Offer to help set up. Seriously! At least, you're seen helping out. So what if people think you're with the hotel or facility crew. What a surprise later when you tell them, "No, I was just giving a hand!" This gives people the impression that you are a roll-up your sleeves kind of guy and not afraid of work. It could pay off.

Familiarize yourself with everyone and everything early on. If you plan to market your business, be shrewd. Stay focused. Keep your eyes open.

Competition may be listening. Arriving early gives you a competitive edge because you've allowed time to size up who the attendees are and how you will approach them.

By arriving early, you also have a chance to introduce yourself to the host before others arrive. At this time, you can offer to be of some assistance. You will earn recognition and appreciation for doing so. Don't be surprised if someone walks up to you and asks, "Are you with XYZ Company?" You can reply, "No, I'm just helping out, what's your name?" Small talk soon turns into what you do, what they do, and exchanging more information with a little time to spare because you went early.

At a minimum, assign yourself the "job" as official greeter, or walk around the room, and ask how people are doing. This will give you the opportunity to speak to people without any pressure.

Never turn your back to the door. Observe the people who enter the networking meeting. Smile as they walk in. They'll feel good about meeting you. Show that you are self-assured, relaxed and easy to approach!

Take a leadership role. A good networker can take on a role as unofficial host. Help others get introduced to others. If you've already met people at the event, and you see someone walk in that hasn't met anyone, step up and introduce them. "Hi, welcome ... what's your name? Would you like me to introduce you to some of the people here? Okay, over there, that's Susan, she's a publicist offering services to those looking to get into publicity ... Over there, that's John, he's a seminar instructor, teaching people how to put on seminars. That's Mary over there, she's into real estate and always looking to help people get into real estate, and over there ..." By standing near the front door, you meet all kinds of people just walking in. By helping to introduce them to people in the room, it makes them feel at ease about meeting new people. You now look like a hero in their eyes and your efforts will not go unappreciated.

Position yourself in a corner where you can see people walk into the event. Get a lay of the landscape by observing where people go within the room ... how they operate. This information can serve you later.

Take a guest along with you that might also benefit from

getting out and meeting new people. Attend with someone who is more extroverted than you are if you feel like you need moral support. (No one ever said that networking is easy.) It's less stressful to travel with others. You can take turns introducing each other. Allow your friend to speak about your strengths while you speak about theirs. A dynamic duo can approach others as a team to ensure you've met everyone, especially if a large group is in attendance.

Seek out introverts. Not everyone is outgoing like you. Some people feel more comfortable hanging back, until asked to join a group. Introverts are not hard to spot because they have a tendency to camouflage themselves in a room! If you are an introvert, use it to your advantage. Approach someone who appears to be as uncomfortable as you are. Even small talk, gives you the opportunity to "practice" networking with others and can actually help you both to develop confidence and make your way around the group. Suggest that you network together as a team.

What To Do <u>DURING</u> The Networking Event

Establish Rapport From The Get-Go!

Rapport is another word for getting along really well with others from a number of levels: physically, emotionally, and subconsciously. The sooner you can establish compatibility with other networkers, the sooner they'll become more comfortable with you and hopefully, continue conversing to the point of leads, sales or some action.

Remember, **people like doing business with people they "trust".** Here are some tips to help you establish rapport with others from the onset:

1) Stand or make subtle gestures in a similar manner as they. Doing this is called "matching" and "mirroring." You match and mirror their physical behaviors. If they fold their arms, you subtly fold your arms. If they cross their legs, you casually do the same. Don't be obvious about what you are doing, of course, then, it looks more like mimicking. Mirroring, however, can be very effective as the other person establishes a comfort level with you, subconsciously and almost immediately.

Speak in a tone similar to the other person. If the person is soft-spoken, lower your voice and talk in a tempo and tonality that matches theirs. This is another subtle way to engage the other person without feeling threatened by a booming voice, as an example.

Breathe in and out in harmony if you can. Relax and help others to relax, too. Exhibit a sense of calm with your own breathing and watch them follow along subconsciously.

Focus by looking directly at the person speaking. Never take your eyes off of the speaker. Pay attention and demonstrate genuine interest in what is being said and be ready to respond to any question. There's nothing worse than having to ask someone to repeat what they said because you weren't listening.

Use similar words they use. Speak their language! Don't talk above them or out of their league. Use words they will understand. Use words and phrases that are meaningful.

Ask open-ended questions. This allows the other person to fully express themselves when asked for information. This will help them appreciate your patience and willingness to listen. Your respect for others will be noticeable. You are no longer a stranger to anyone that meets you. You become the go-to-person that everyone will want to meet.

Direct the conversation in a way that benefits your audience without them realizing it. A sample response from you might be: "I know, and what if you did _____ to improve _____ ..." Your offer to assist with business suggestion gets people listening when they know the information will help them. Focus on their comments and questions to keep the conversation flowing. The interest you show in others is noticed and appreciated. Everyone likes to feel like they are making a valuable contribution.

What Else Should You Know & Do During A Networking Event So You Maximize Your Time Spent?

If you press to soon, you might lose a deal. Let people's needs come to you *from them*. Introduce yourself, ask a few easy, open-ended questions to start the conversation; listen; observe; be patient and prepared to respond and then use the information with careful precision. When you feel like you really know the person, you're in a good position to advise them with *surgical precision*.

Don't discuss money, sales or selling too soon. Think of it like this: For every second you talk money too soon, you will lose a dollar in perceived value or other perception in the end. Don't be in such a rush to talk price, your fees, etc. Build value first for your product/service. Talk benefits and stories. Describe in detail all the work you have done for clients and can do for them. When you eventually do talk about costs, the customer sees the value right away. "Hands down, this is a good deal ... count me in! Can you take payment with your phone? Do you take credit cards?"

Have patience. Timing is everything. If you ask too soon, you won't get anything. Maybe you are in need of a special favor. The golden Rule is, let other people come to you because they want to. ATTRACT THEM by listening and showing yourself to be the real deal; an expert in your field. Knowing WHEN to ask is an art. The balances must always be equal or at least lean in their favor. What can you do for them (before you ask for what you need) so that when you do ask, you have a greater chance of getting what you ask for?

Your stealth-like mannerisms, conversations, eye contact, body language ... are big sellers! You're never aggressive, never in people's faces or space, never interrupting, never attempt to finish the statements of others behaving like some know-it-all. You walk tall, with certainty, and poised to do good business.

In fact, **you want people to "come to you"**. Step back and think about your next move. See if people seek you out of the crowd when they know you just entered the room to network with others.

Ask to be introduced to others. This helps to get the networking momentum moving in your direction! Ask a friend or the host at the event, "Who have you met tonight? Anyone exciting that you can introduce me to or recommend I meet? I'd appreciate an introduction!"

Again, your attitude when networking should be a little ... *stealth-like!* Networking and socializing with others is fun, but you're also there for business. Remember your agenda for the evening, your goals, etc. You're there to learn what others do, and to see if there's anyone in the crowd you'd like to work with. Don't be too eager to work with everyone you meet. Filter out those who are not good prospects. Lay low and let folks welcome and persuade you to join their groups. This can be very effective.

Be a leader and project leadership qualities. Introduce new people to others that have already arrived. Help the host if they need help and remember to take plenty of pictures for your website's press room page and to share with other attendees.

Be fun, energetic, full of life and spontaneous. Never let people guess what you'll do next. I have a saying when it comes to marketing and selling to customers, which can be applied to networking with people ... "Always leave your customers wanting more. Never leave them fully satisfied!" It means, never give too much information about you and what you do. Withhold a little to keep those you meet wanting more from you. This leaves them even more curious and wanting to pursue you later. They might really looking forward to talking with you after the event, more than any other person they met there!

Be prepared to accept orders for your products. Have order forms ready. Experiment with different sizes: full page, 1/2 page, 1/4 page size, etc. and go with what's easier for people to complete quickly. Have change on hand ($1's, $5's, $10's and $20's). Have business cards with your web address on them so people know where to order your products after the event. Do you have a merchant account so you can accept credit card orders? Do you have a credit card swiper for your phone, such as PayPal and Square? There's also Venmo and Cash.me (apps) that allows people to send you cash, which you can then deposit right into your bank account.

Be the last person out the door. Seize the opportunity to learn as much as you can from every person unless the event doesn't meet your needs. Do not waste valuable time networking with the wrong people.

Be seen, but not heard! This is a networking tactic where people may have seen you at an event (i.e., at your table, walking around, talking to others, etc.), but missed the opportunity to speak with you. This adds to the mystique or celebrity-like role you play when networking. *"I saw him/her there, but I didn't get a chance to meet that person! Next time, I'm not going to miss the chance to meet everyone!"*

Bring something special to the event to make you stand out. This could be anything from baked goods people might enjoy; a magic trick, prop or other *gimmick* that makes you stand out among the crowd when networking. Keep it professional.

If you don't already know, I make some of the world's best chocolate chip cookies and sell them on one of my websites. Sometimes, I'll take a batch to a networking event where I know the meeting planner, speaker, attendees or the host of the event. On one occasion, the event coordinator allowed me to pass my cookies out to the attendees as she proceeded to introduce me to every single one of them. It was a small group of about 20 people at the event. Not only did I get to meet everyone, but I also left a lasting impression on them just by handing out my cookies. You can learn more about my famous chocolate chip cookies at ***BartsCookies.com***. You might also check out ***iLoveBartsCookies.com*** to read what others think about them. Don't just take my word for it.

So, here's your homework: Come up with your own gimmick, trick, tip or prop and take it to the next networking event you attend so you stand out in the crowd. Don't think you won't be remembered for that personal touch and making the effort because you will.

Never attend an event without business cards or your information quickly available to send someone via text. Give them out discreetly, of course. You might even design one yourself and just take a picture of it. Then, when someone asks for your card, just send them the digital version to their phone from yours. Most cards get thrown away anyway, so just send yours virtually.

Do not leave people alone. A good networker can act as an unofficial host. Basically, it's just helping others to meet people, especially if you can point them in the right direction. Don't be a bystander when you are surrounding by so much potential business whether it is in the form of contacts, leads, or sales.

Heard, but not seen! People heard you were there, speaking, networking, manning a table, etc., but they didn't get to meet you or even see you at large event. This builds more mystique and intrigue about you. Your name is buzzing throughout the groups and people are saying good things about you. That's powerful in building your brand and "celebrity" status in your industry. "I've heard so much about (name)! Where can I find him/her? If you see (name), will you find me? I would like to get an autograph on his/her book that I just purchased!" Do you see what I mean?

Help the host. You will earn points, global recognition, and thanks in the form of gifts, special introductions, lunch/dinner invitations, etc. Plan to introduce yourself to every speaker (and host) at an event. Volunteer to help the host meet and greet people who come into the event. It's a great way to meet everyone anyway. No, you're not part of the staff, which you tell people, but they're delighted someone is welcoming them. Help the host set up and/or take down their event table, posters, displays and easels.

Move in or move on! Get what you need and move on. Do not monopolize people's time and don't let others monopolize yours. Networking is an opportunity to learn as much as you can in the shortest amount of time. Talk at length later, on the phone or in person, at the office or other location.

Not seen and not heard! Here's a situation where you're not at an event and your personal name or company name isn't mentioneed either. The good, the bad and the ugly ... The GOOD: You don't want or need to be seen or heard at that event so you don't go.

Great. You'd rather attend events that are worth more of your time to go to. The BAD: Maybe you could give it one more try? If you did go, you might get some business, you might not. The UGLY: By NOT going, you're not making an impact on people (directly or indirectly). So, what do you do? Don't be afraid to NOT show up to a particular event, no matter the size or popularity of it, IF it doesn't benefit you. You know this, I'm sure, but it's important to weigh the pros and cons of attending or not attending networking events. Because you aren't seen/heard at an event and you eventually do decide to attend, wow, perhaps people are pleasantly surprised by your attendance and spend a little more time talking to you. You just never know.

Observe how the networking event is set up, so you can host your own event in the future. Learn how people interact. What kinds of activities are there to reinforce the meet and greet to ensure people get what they need? What food and drinks do people like at these events? How about the building, location, time of day, weekday or weekend? Knowing the process for setting up a networking event, what to do and what not to do, can help you to create a successful networking experience for yourself and others.

Really work the room! Exhaust every opportunity to speak with as many people as possible. Pick up every piece of literature for study or follow-up purposes. Make yourself known to as many people as possible.

Seen and heard. This is the most obvious action item at any networking event ... to be seen and heard by everyone in the room. You've made your presence known; people enjoyed talking to you; and you're a master networker in their eyes. The next time the event takes place, and you're not there? Whoa! That's a loss for that event and people feel it. You (always) leave such a good impression with people at every event you attend, that people ask where you are when you're not there. Don't be surprised to get phone calls and text messages from people asking you, will you come to the next event?

What about drinks? Know the rules. Drink in moderation or not at all so YOU remain focused and can navigate the room without looking like a fool or talking too loud or worse, with alcohol on your breath. Remember, you're talking to people up close. Plus, you want to get home safely after the event if you drove.

Smile, Smile, Smile! Smiling connects us with people. As one of the universal languages, it spreads joy and comfort! Especially if you plan to socialize, brush those teeth, freshen that breath and keep smiling to attract more of the same energy right back.

DO turn your cell phone off or put it on "vibrate." No exceptions! If you're expecting a call, keep it on vibrate and put the phone in your pocket. Ring tones are intrusive and interruptive. If you must check a "vibrating" call, excuse yourself from the group to check on it.

Do not pull out your cell phone to see who the caller is. If you must talk on the phone, go outside of the room for privacy and out of respect for others. There are no excuses for cell phone abuse. The cell phone abuses that bothers you will bother others. Show good cell-phone-manners at all times! If you're expecting someone to call you, you'll know if it's vibrating! ... *Bzzzzzzzz ... Bzzzzzzzz!*

Avoid being in anyone's space. Allow people to approach you by making yourself available and open to questions and conversation. Don't monopolize anyone's space or conversation or overstay your welcome. Keep moving.

Commit to introducing yourself to five new people and reconnect with five others you already know (at a minimum). Don't under utilize the time you spend at a networking event.

If promotion tables have been set up, visit all of them. Collect marketing material, literature, and business cards and don't hesitate to leave your information with the people hosting those tables. Even if you think you might not be interested in the literature you pick up, you might get some great ideas from the content, style, and more. The courtesy could pay off later.

Business Dining Etiquette

Good breakfast/lunch/dinner table etiquette will always make a valued impression. Let common sense be your guide, and watch others if you are faced with a situation where you really don't know what to do. Bad manners will also leave a lasting impression.

As soon as you **sit down, place your napkin on your lap**. Then, look over the menu and place your order. Get the ordering (of food and drink) out of the way first. This helps the restaurant staff to keep things moving for them. Then, proceed to discussing business without interruption.

If you have to **get up, fold your napkin neatly and place it beside your plate** where it was originally placed, on the left side.

Gentlemen, when a lady arrives at the table or gets up to leave the table stand up to greet her or respect her leaving the table. You might assist ladies into their chairs or take their coats. Chivalry isn't dead! Good manners never go out of style.

It goes without saying, **don't eat too fast, don't chew with your mouth open**, don't speak with your mouth full, and don't make noises while you're eating. It's RUDE! People will move away from you if you are discourteous and you can lose big time.

Silverware is typically placed in the order it will be used. Not sure which utensil to use? The rule is to work from the outside in. Observe others for direction. If everyone seems awkward, just do your best.

Once you use a utensil (knife, fork), do not set it back down on the tablecloth. Keep it on the plate. The knife should rest at the top of the plate or a place it on your bread plate if you have one. When you have finished a meal, place your silverware on the plate to signal to the waiter that you are ready to have the plate picked up. Some waiters will ask you to keep your fork because dessert is coming. Ask for a clean one. That's my tip!

Don't hesitate to ask for a new fork, spoon or knife throughout the meal. Generally, you will be provided with the precise utensils that you will need for the order you requested. Use your soup spoon for soup and not to stir your coffee. If you aren't provided with a clean fork, knife or spoon when you change courses, ask.

What about alcohol? If no one orders an alcoholic drink, don't order one either. If others do order alcoholic drinks, it is recommended that you don't. It shows that you are more interested in the conversation. If you'd like to have a drink, you can always order one after the networking event.

If hors d'œuvres are served, have only a few. I've seen people load up with the excuse that he/she missed dinner. It's RUDE and besides you don't want to be eating or juggling a plate of food when you are trying to make a pitch! Bad manners will always get attention, but not the kind you want.

Don't linger around "social traps" such as the bar or the buffet. These are comfortable places for people to congregate! Not for you! Once you consume a little food or drink, get back to networking. Keep moving!

When eating bread, don't pick up the entire roll, or even half of it. Break a small piece off and butter it at your plate. Use the bread plate if you have one. After you butter it, place your knife down on the plate, and take a small bite of the bread. Don't hold your knife in one hand and your bread in the other. Seriously, remember to break the bread/roll and do not slice it down the middle with your knife then butter both sides. Improper etiquette is a dead give-away.

Don't rearrange the name cards on the table. If you want to sit next to someone, tell the host prior to the event or ask the person you're sitting next to if you can change seats! Or, sit at a new table that has an open seat.

Who should pay the bill? This will depend on who extended the invitation. Typically, that person will pay the check. If you are the recipient, don't forget to return the favor. In other situations, it's always best to either offer to split the bill or pay your own way. Consider asking for separate checks, especially if you're dining with a large crowd. Large crowds have a tendency to hide an abusive spender. So, protect your wallet!

If you need to leave the group to visit the rest room or run to your car, don't leave your purse or briefcase unattended. Take it with you unless you wisely placed it in the trunk of your car beforehand. If you have these items with you when you leave the table, ask someone you trust to protect your items. For security, always take your wallet with credit cards and driver's license, even your laptop if you are concerned about propriety information, with you. Never leave your laptop unattended for any reason. That goes for cameras and other electronic equipment as well. It's been known to happen, but the employees of hotels and other facilities have easy access into rooms and quick access out! A wise rule to follow would be to take responsibility for your personal/business property. Trust no one and suspect everyone.

Know when to LEAVE — be the last one out the door. Watch as people begin to leave an event. Towards the end, you usually have more time to speak with them more openly about themselves, business, their needs and yours. At that time, most folks aren't overwhelmed with the 15 or 75 people trying to get to them. It's also a great time to spend with the hosts or speakers of the event and get their feedback based on their networking experiences! Who knows what joint venture opportunities will arise when the event is winding down and you can get to the heart of some of your questions. If they seem too busy to talk then help out anyone. It could improve your chances for engagement.

Who knows, maybe they've been waiting to speak to you and now's the perfect time, since you are willing to stick around! Plus, by helping, you earn extra points and are remembered and appreciated. You will have made a great connection.

Watch The Clock!

Keep an eye on the time for all of these reasons:

1. **Where did you park your car?** Did you fund the meter long enough to take advantage of free parking after a certain time? Did you read what time that was? Does the parking meter need more money? Did you get your parking ticket validated or get

that coupon they were offering for a discount off parking? Many residential areas have specified parking limits. Read the signs before you park. In all these cases, watch the clock!

2. **You'll want to make sure you speak to every person** before they leave the event. So, watch the clock!

3. **You'll want to be sure you take pictures of certain people** before the event ends and/or during the event. Ask people before they leave if they'd like to be in a photo with you. Not everyone likes to have their picture taken. Don't wait too long because you may not be aware of when they leave.

4. **Plan your purchases** before the event is over. Make sure you visit specific tables and vendors at the event before they close their promotion tables down or run out of product.

5. **You might want to visit other vendor tables** you didn't get to see earlier while networking. Use this opportunity to get new ideas and to see what people are buying and why.

6. **Hungry?** Make sure your group gets out before the restaurants close in the hotel, around town, etc. In most cases, all you need is to get your order in before the kitchen closes at the restaurant you want to go to. They might be closing in 10-15 minutes, but most restaurants let folks hang out about an hour afterwards.

7. **If your networking goes later than expected, and you have someone special waiting for you,** do call to reassure him/her that the event is almost over and when you can be expected. Then, call again to let the person know you are leaving, provided the person hasn't gone to bed. Your call will be appreciated.

Other Networking Notes

Polish your business etiquette and protocol. Always, be on your best behavior. Read up on books and websites that offer insight on proper etiquette. People are attracted to and will welcome doing business with "class acts" such as yourself.

Selectively distribute your business cards. Don't think that you must give out everyone your business cards. *Be selective.* On the other hand, don't hesitate to ask for most cards from others. You never know when someone asks you for a referral and while you cannot personally help out, you have a card of someone that can. Ask card owners about their business and hobbies. Keep them talking so you can assess whether or not they'd be someone you'd actually like *doing business with.* It gives you time to decide if they're good prospects.

Take notes when you're at a networking event. When you return to your table or during the next break, write a note on the back of the business cards to remind you of specific details about your meeting.

Networking Tactics For Attending & Working Trade Shows

Walk by every table in the room/building/event. Don't miss a thing. Even if there are a hundred tables that last aisle might contain the most valuable contact or information literature for you. Remember, these events come and go. Make the most of your opportunity to network at these shows particularly if it's a competitor's show.

Pick up any literature that gives you ideas for marketing, packaging, design, content, joint venture ideas, etc. Take something to carry all the papers, folders, brochures and business cards you will accumulate. Don't be shy either! Pick up all the literature that speaks to you. Even if you're not interested in the products/services, get some good "design" examples for your own brochure or postcard. Always say, "Thank you!"

Speak with vendors. Inquire about placing some of your flyers/business cards on other vendor's tables. Perhaps, they might be interested in joining your affiliate program and selling some of your products or services. Can <u>their</u> products and services be of interest to your clients, prospects and affiliates? If so, then you just made a great new contact! Ask for their name and contact information. Maybe you can assist each other. Reassure him/her that you'll be calling soon to follow-up on your conversation.

Talk with other attendees. These people are there for the same reasons you are -- to meet people to do business with! Find out what they do and why they're attending this particular event. Keep the conversation directed toward them. If you're interested in continuing the conversations, ask for their telephone numbers, business cards and prepare to move on.

Before you "move on," acknowledge what you have in common and establish that you would like to meet again to further the idea of doing business together. Just because the conversation is over, it doesn't mean you're done. You want to sustain a positive impression, so follow-up is vital. Always make sure to send a text or email to remind a person that you will be calling. Reference something that was discussed or piece of advice he/she gave. Ask to connect on LinkedIn. Be sure to follow up ASAP. Then move on to your next prospect.

Attending Networking Events or Trade Shows WITH Table/Booth

Attract people to your booth with a professional appearance and some kind of gimmick! Attractive banners (in front and behind your table), display designs on easels, props, posters (on the wall or on easels) and laptop/computer screen to show and tell people about your products or your website and if you can offer a sample of your products on display, you'll get the attention you want.

Check out **MyTrainingCenter.com** for trade show marketing tactics, checklists for what to have at your trade show table and how to set up your trade show table to maximize marketing and networking with others.

Draw attention by using magnets to your table such as food, candy, balloons, a clown -- anything to get people around your booth. Form a crowd around your booth, and you'll get gold mine of prospects. How do you do this? I once made my famous chocolate chip cookies (**BartsCookies.com**) and took them to a women's business expo where I had a table. The deal that I offered was a cookie for a card! I made out like a bandit! Plus, people started tasting my cookies at the event and began to refer other people to my table. The cookies were gone by the end of the day and I had a plenty of business cards to enter into my prospect database.

Collect names/eMail addresses! Offer something for free in exchange for names and eMail addresses. Place a bowl on the table to collect business cards. Create short name/eMail forms that people can fill out if they don't have business cards. Offer a prize drawing (on the hour, two a day, daily, etc.) and put a list out for so they can register for it with all of their contact information. Most people will sign up if a free gift is offered. Let people know that you'll announce the winner by eMail, so remind them to write clearly on the form.

Stand in front of your table! Don't sit/stand behind your table/booth. Get out in front of it to greet people as they walk by. Engage them in conversation. Get people talking and don't miss the opportunities to tell your story and to show your products.

Hand out materials in the aisle! Stand in front of your booth and distribute postcards, flyers, brochures and business cards. Later on in the day, that person who never took a moment to stop or saw your booth, may go through your literature and decide to return! You can imagine them reading your brochure, flyer or business card over their lunch break, and here he/ she comes. So, don't hide behind your trade show table. It creates a physical and psychological barrier between you and potential customer. You are more approachable to a stranger (or a prospect) if you're on the same side of the table.

Be sure to list your booth/table number on your website, literature, and more in case someone wants to find you, for example, "VISIT US AT TABLE #20."

Organize your table with appropriately placed plastic display cases! Make sure you have the right size and number of plastic display cases to show your flyers, brochures and business cards. It helps when you can focus your time on talking to prospects and you don't have to shuffle through papers and flyers looking for the information you wanted to give. I like to have 1, 2 and 3 level flyer display holders, a single or multi-level business card holder, and a postcard display holder. An attractive table attracts people!

Check out **MyTrainingCenter.com** for trade show marketing tactics, checklists for what to have at your trade show table and specifically how to set up your trade show table.

Talk to other vendors! Take time to speak with other vendors (in the next booth, across the aisle and more. Don't miss an chances to make new contacts even if they are the competition! If you're working a booth with a friend or business partner; have the other person watch your table, while you walk down the aisles checking other vendors. If you're alone, then the first thing you need to do is introduce yourself to your neighboring vendors. Later, you may feel comfortable asking one of them to watch your booth while you explore the event. You can certainly return the favor.

Use a small speaker microphone to be heard above the noise especially if you are in a large setting! This works well, indoors and outdoors, when you wish to give a presentation on your product/service and you want people to be heard. Done with courtesy to other vendors, it is an acceptable form of communication at many networking events. You can captivate the attention of attendees by telling your story, live! Check with the event planner for the rules and regulations on using a microphone.

Protect your personal and business belongings! Keep your wallet, car keys and identification on you. Don't risk losing them, because someone swiped your briefcase or purse when you weren't looking. If you're traveling out of town, definitely take extra precautions. Make copies of your credit cards and driver's license and keep them in a safe place (trunk of your car, glove box, etc.). Leave valuables at your hotel or with the hotel manager, or just don't travel with items such as expensive jewelry and large sums of cash. Remember, you're among hundreds, maybe thousands of strangers. Better to be safe than sorry.

Continue To Improve Your Observation Skills!

With time, **constantly improving your "observation skills" will help you become a sharper,** more alert networking master.

Who should you be observing? People. How do they approach you, talk to you, carry themselves, dress (professionally or casually), body language, react to your small talk, respond to questions, behave in a crowd of people or alone, address others and anything else that will help you become a better judge of character. Constantly improve how you read people you meet. They may be good prospects and good customers.

Why observe people? Observing how people live, act and react in life and in business will help you make important decisions about whether you can work with them or not.

Know When To Leave

In many cases, it could prove advantageous to be the last person out the door. Toward the end of the event, you usually have more time to speak with people more candidly without interruption or feeling overwhelmed by groups of people.

If the event was a bust and you've made only a few introductions, you'd be wise to pack up. Time is money, even when networking. Think carefully about why the event wasn't successful. Are there any things you might have done differently? How can you improve your performance or better showcase your information? Would you consider the event well attended? Why? Why not?

You must always be weighing your strengths and weaknesses carefully so that you can continue to build an effective strategy to achieve your networking goals.

What To Do AFTER The Networking Event

When the event is about to close, this is the time to spend some *quality time* with the hosts, any speakers, key contacts you made at the event. Here are some opening lines to rekindle conversations:

> **"... How did it go tonight?"**

> **"... Great night! What did you think?"**

"... Do you have a minute to chat before you go?"

"... Can I help you pack up?"

"... When's the next networking event?"

"... I wanted to talk to you about working together."

"... I wanted to find out if I could promote your site and if you might be interested in promoting mine?"

"... Do you need speakers at events like these?"

"... What does it take to have a table at this event?"

"... May I leave some literature with you for the next event?

Get feedback. Always ask for feedback to determine if you are an effective networker. Ask a trustworthy person to give you feedback on your performance at the event.

Did people seem to enjoy meeting you? Did they ask questions about you? What was the overall interest from the people who met you? Be prepared to make appropriate changes in your networking style or behavior.

Organize the business cards you received from people at the networking event. Whatever system you use, be sure that you can readily access them when you return to your home or office.

Upon leaving, check to make sure you have everything. Make certain that you have your car keys, wallet, purse, laptop (if you brought one), briefcase, any products, order forms, etc. It's easy to leave something behind. This is where a checklist is helpful. Don't expect to recover anything you left behind particularly if the event took place in a high traffic area, public building or a hotel. If you do, then you're lucky!

Thank everyone. Thank the host, the event coordinators, hotel/ facility manager and staff. Saying "thank you" comes back to you in ways you can't imagine. Good manners go a long way in making that lasting impression.

Wash your hands before you go to your car. No doubt, you've been shaking hands with a lot of people. Before you head to the car, visit the washroom to wash your hands and face. Seriously! You'll feel fresh and clean driving home or back to the office.

On your way home or back to the office, reflect on the networking event. Who made the biggest impression on you? What did you learn from those you met? What appointments would you like to set up right away? Make plans to do this while your conversations with people are still fresh in your mind and in theirs.

When the time is right, **call a few key contacts and tell them about the networking event you attended**. Ask if they got any new ideas or new contacts or anything they can share with you that would be helpful? Share your enthusiasm for the event and any prospects. There may be even more opportunities to work together.

When you share all this wonderful news, your excitement will shine through the phone to the other person, getting them excited too! Who knows what kind of business can be generated off that kind of excitement, new ideas, new contacts, etc. Wow, get busy!

Stay in touch with new leads, affiliates, clients and associates you met at the networking event. In the next section, we'll go over specific ways you can maintain your relationships and take your network to all new heights!

NETWORKING COMPONENT #10

FUTURE GROWTH

How Do You Continue To Grow Your Business & Income By Networking?

People will do more business with you when they (1) **see you often**, (2) **know that you are resourceful**, and (3) **stay in touch** with them on a regular basis by telephone, eMail, social media, and/or in-person.

Following a networking event, nurture your new contacts and prospects. Follow up with them to develop the business relationships you added to your portfolio.

Prioritizing Leads & Prospects

1. **SORT YOUR LEADS into three distinct categories:**

   HOT: These are the people with whom you have arranged to contact because your contacts want information and you are optimistic about creating a business relationship with them.

   WARM: These are the people who potentially could do business with you in the future, but you have no strong reason to contact them immediately.

   COLD: These are the people whom you have no direct connection with and who probably cannot provide you with a service or product.

2. **TAKE ACTION with the cards you collected:**

   HOT: Contact each person and arrange to meet them for a more fact-finding meeting. Drop off information if requested. Personal deliveries make a good impression. Above all, get the appointment. Be creative.

   WARM: Send an eMail to each person, reminding him/her where you met and what you discussed. Stay focused on the highlights and benefits your product and/or service could offer them. Look for commonalities in your businesses to establish a comfort level as you begin the process of developing your business relationships.

COLD: While there may be no reason to enter these leads into your database, you never know when one of your friends, customers, clients, or contacts could use their help. So, for that reason, choose to enter them now or not at all.

Organize Your Business Cards

Organize the cards you have categorized by (a) potential customer, (b) affiliate/referral partner, (c) vendor, (d) general, etc. Follow up on the first two as soon as possible. Don't wait!

Follow-Up Immediately!

Has this ever happened to you? You meet someone at a professional meeting, exchange business cards, and suggest that you follow-up with each other, and then you neglect to make the call. Two weeks later, even the note you wrote on the back of the business card doesn't trigger your memory.

It is important to follow-up immediately (certainly within 24-72 hours or sooner) while the person and the conversation are current in your minds. Don't waste time. Follow up only with contacts you met and are interested in working with unless someone gives you a referral. Don't skip a beat. Make that call!

Put each person you met into your database and then send a personalized note or message by phone or by eMail. Keep it short and professional to trigger their memory. Suggest a meeting to further discuss the possibilities of doing business together. Something as simple as getting together for lunch or coffee is absolutely an ideal first step.

If you are serious about a business appointment, suggest a meeting soon after your introduction to discuss your proposal. Be prepared with details to discuss how you both will benefit from the venture you suggest.

Options For Follow Up

1. Follow up with a simple eMail. An eMail is an expedient way to make a connection with someone that you hope to continue speaking with. Ask the person to recommend a good time to meet over the next few days. Generally, people will be pleased to hear from you and hopefully you beat them to it! It shows interest and earnest. Why? How many people do you know that will make the time to religiously follow up on their contacts and actually get the appointments?

As soon as you get home or back to the office following a networking event, choose three to five people that you'd like to contact because you believe there is potential for your business? Send them an eMail to let them know it was a pleasure meeting them and you'd like to continue your discussion following the networking event. Here's a suggested eMail message format:

> **Hey _____,**
>
> **Iit was a pleasure meeting you last night at (company name) networking event. I particularly enjoyed our conversation regarding _____.**
>
> **We have a lot in common. I'd like to continue our discussion on _____. Would lunch or a meeting at one of our offices work best for you? Let me know your best time. I look forward to hearing from you soon.**
>
> **Best regards,**
> **(Your Name)**

You can see how simple it is to send a quick note! If you are sending an eMail or personal note, why not attach the photograph of you and the other person from the event. Wouldn't that make an impression?

2. Follow up with a message you might send to them via SOCIAL MEDIA. Do they have a LinkedIn or Facebook account?

Can you find them and connect with them or Friend them? Like their fan page and then send them a message, such as:

> **"Hey _____, it was a pleasure meeting you at last night's networking event. I particularly enjoyed talking to you about _____. I'm very interested in continuing that dialogue. Got time for a phone call this week? Let me know what works best for you ... (Your Name)"**

People are pleasantly surprised when they hear from people they met at networking events, because? NO ONE ever follows up. Well, only a handful ever do. Not you. You always make sure you continue to grow your new friendships and prospects.

3. Follow up with a TELEPHONE CALL. Even if you have sent an eMail, follow up with a phone call to the key people you met at the event to keep it personal. These calls are not sales calls. You're just checking in to determine if they too would be interested in doing business with you based on your discussion at the networking event.

You might want to do business with them, but they might not want to do business with you. Either way, you'll never know, unless you call. So, here's a sample script you could use when contacting someone by telephone having met them while networking.

> **"Hi, _____, this is _____, how are you? We met at the _____ networking event last night (or the other night). It was a pleasure meeting you. Is this a good time to call?** *(Offer to set up a time to call back if the person is busy. Take control by suggesting a time to continue the conversation.)* **I wanted to talk to you about your company, and some of the things I am working on that might be of interest to you ... Based on what you shared at the event last night, I thought it would be a great idea to ..."** *(And, proceed to talk business!)*

4. Follow up by SIGNING UP to RECEIVE THEIR ONLINE NEWSLETTER or EZINE or subscribe to their PODCAST or YOUTUBE (or other) channel. Contact the individuals personally by eMail or telephone to let them know that you will contact them. Take an interest in people you network with by signing up to receive their content, whether it's audio, video, a newsletter, etc. It gives you a frame of reference when you speak to them. Showing interest in others (with action) can lay the foundation for business opportunities.

"Hi, it's (your name). I met you at last night's networking event. I just subscribed to you _____ today. I look forward to what I can learn. I am also interested in discussing the material I gave you at the event. I know it complements what your company has to offer. Would you like to schedule a time to talk about that potential? Would you prefer to meet in person or cover this over the phone?"

5. Follow up by PURCHASING ONE OF THEIR PRODUCTS from their website. Maybe the person you met also wrote a book. Why not buy the book, read it and comment about it with the author on the phone? Or, offer a review of the book and give positive feedback.

"Hi, this is (your name). I bought your book and I'd like to give you a testimonial. Would you be interested in having lunch or a phone conversation where we go over that and some of my ideas for how we might be able to work together? What day/time is good for you? Would Wednesday or Thursday work? *(Always give the person one of two choices versus suggesting sometime next week. It pins the person down to make a decision.)* If I bring your book will you autograph it? Thanks, Wednesday it is ... see you then."

6. Follow up by JOINING THEIR AFFILIATE PROGRAM. This is another great way to contact people after you just met them. Join their affiliate program so you both can make money! AWESOME!

> "Hello, it's (Your Name) ... We met last night at the networking event. I was viewing your website and thought my customers would be interested in your products/services, so I signed up to become one of your affiliates. I'll be making an announcement about your products/services to my list next week that will include a reference to your website through my affiliate link. I believe we can make some money. I'd like to interview you too. Would that be possible?" *(Then suggest a time when you both can talk about your ideas.)*

If you take a genuine interest in others, they'll take an interest in you. If you can generate business for them, that gives them incentive to help you, too!

Other Ways To Grow Your Business Into The Future By Networking

Serve on charity boards, local organizations, business associations, social groups, and attend more networking events.

Start your own networking group. Create an account at MeetUp.com and/or use EventBrite.com for event registrations. Invite people to bring someone new each week to share ideas, share stories, trade phone numbers and refer business. Charge a small fee or conduct free events because you value the potential of the contacts you will all make!

Turn all meetings and events into networking opportunities. You knew that one, right? Don't think twice about distributing your business cards, postcards or flyers when appropriate.

Stay In Touch — Always!

There are several ways to maintain contact with people you meet at networking events. When you get home, enter their names, phone numbers, and eMail addresses into your contact database. If you have their permission, you could put them on your mailing list to receive information about you and your products and services on a regular basis. This is a good marketing tactic especially when a person isn't quite ready for an initial proposal to *"let's talk about how we can work together."* Instead, this let's them get to know you over time. This keeps them in the loop with what you're up to and when ready, they'll reach out to you.

Out Of Sight — Out Of Mind!

Don't allow too much time to pass you by after meeting new contacts. Out of sight really is *out of mind!* If you can't schedule a meeting within a week of meeting them, at least send the individual a text or eMail letting them know you're looking forward to talking with them soon and making an appointment to meet.

Don't leave scheduling that important appointment up to the other person. No, that's your job to ensure you two meet. Like destiny, never let anyone else control yours. You take the reigns and make sure you both meet up or have that phone call. Besides, this goes a long way to you respecting your time.

Make Periodic Calls & Send Messages & Emails To Check In!

When too much time has elapsed and you haven't heard from a contact, place another call or eMail a note to the effect that you're just checking in to see how they're doing. Keep it short, but genuine. Ask if you can be of any assistance to them. Recommend a meeting time if it seems like you peaked their interest.

> **"Hey, how are things going? I haven't spoken with you in a while and wanted to check in. Hope everything's good. What's new and exciting in your world that you'd like to share? I'm all ears!"**

This is your chance to update the person with what you've been doing. Reconnect and watch business pick up again. Seek out those you've helped in the past that you know should be pleased to get a call or eMail and receptive to renewing your business relationship.

Reach out to all your past clients for follow up. Who knows what new opportunities you might find? They might need you again and they appreciate hearing from you. They might have a new lead for you. They might just be glad you thought enough to call. Who knows when a new lead or sale or request for assistance won't develop in the near future?

Periodically, Reconnect With Your Network — Don't Be A Stranger!

Call or eMail key contacts with an update about your recent projects about what you're looking to accomplish. Continue to build your database of contacts, manage it well, stay in touch, follow-up often, and never stop networking. Your business depends on it as does theirs.

Treat Your Best Relationships Like Gold!

These people could be the lifeblood of your business. They may be contacting you with referrals, business, leads or tips. Treat them like gold! Stay in touch. Try to remember dates that are important to them such as birthdays, anniversaries, holidays, etc.

Organize Your Own Networking Group

Have you attended many networking events and you're ready to have your own? Can you make any improvements on what you've observed? Why not consider hosting your own networking event? With a little planning, you too can be successful at setting up an opportunity to connect with other business owners or those of like mind and passion. Here's what you do:

1. Decide on a name or theme for your networking event so you can invite people who too can benefit from getting together at your event. Once you have a name for it, you might consider registering a domain name for it. I did. When I came up with *TIME TO NETWORK*, I went and registered the domain for it, TimeToNetwork.com. You might also create a fan page on Facebook for it. For sure, you'll want a place where you can upload photos and video of your events. Until you build a website, why not forward (or redirect) your domain name to your Facebook Fan page? I've done that before. Works great!

2. Find a location for the event. It can be a restaurant, hotel, conference room, even your home or office. Keep it professional. Inquire about the cost of rent a meeting room and the potential for supplying food and beverages. Some shared meeting spaces are completely empty after 5pm and will allow you to use their space if you subscribe to their monthly service, which can be anywhere between $50-$500 a month. If you conduct more than one event per month, this could be worth it.

3. Should you charge a fee for your event? It's your call. However, if you plan to charge attendees, keep the fee at $10-$20 per person. Make it affordable or people won't go. Free is best even if you are provided some type of mini-refreshment. Think of all the potential business. If you decide on a price, you can sell tickets to your event from your website by using **EventBrite.com** to collect the money and send out receipts and directions, as well as calendar notifications for each event you conduct. Instruct attendees to bring the receipt they received via eMail to the event as proof of registration. If you use EventBrite, you can generate a list from all those who registered to assist you with at-the-door registration and administrative needs.

4. Make an announcement on your website or on social media and ask others to do the same to their list. Give yourself about two weeks out to promote the event. DO NOT tell people you're having a networking event this weekend and expect a huge attendance. No one will show with such short notice. You need to allow people a minimum of a week or two to plan ahead for your event. The more time you give people, the more people can schedule time to attend. Also, if you hold them regularly, people will always know to come if they can make it. Remind them a few days before the event and the day of to be sure they know to attend.

Another tip is to post a list of all the people who are planning to attend your event (plus their website addresses) on your website. Encourage your soon-to-be attendees to review the list before they attend to help them put their networking plans together. *"Look who's coming to the event. Check out their websites. Come with questions and ideas for ways you can work together, etc."* What a great way for your guests to break the ice than by knowing who they can expect to meet at your event.

5. When you host your own networking event, spend most of that time working the crowd. Make contact with every attendee. Ensure that everyone's having a good time. This is your networking event and it's important that *you* meet *everyone!* Introduce new people to other attendees. Make the most of your position and keep the networking momentum going.

6. Have a table so attendees can display their products, flyers and business cards. Encourage people to bring them to share, promote and network with the group.

7. After the event is over, contact everyone who attended personally, by phone or eMail. Ask them to share feedback regarding the event and any tips for improvement. Once you receive their (positive) responses, share them on your website on that event page. Have people post on your Facebook fan page what a great time they had to encourage others to come to future events.

ALWAYS, STAY IN TOUCH!

However you communicate with new contacts, it's good to have weekly or bi-monthly communication with them, whether it's by eMail, webinar, tele-seminar, new video, new podcast episode, … whatever. Stay in touch! Out of sight, out of mind. Don't be a stranger. Your ongoing communications update your network with what you're doing, and keeps you at the forefront of their mind as much as possible. Networking is about leveraging your business and personal connections to bring you a regular supply of new leads, contacts, friends, sales and business. To be successful at networking, you must be proactive. Challenge yourself to find new opportunities to network that you might not have considered before. In doing so, you will be making an invaluable investment in the steady growth of your business and in your life.

My Networking Tactics
by Bart Smith, TheMarketingMan.com

CONCLUSION

To be a successful networker, incorporate all of these suggestions into your business and professional activities. By networking regularly with like-minded people, you can help your business stay ahead of the competition.

Networking can be a fun and easy way to enrich your life, broaden your horizons and enhance your career. Crucial to your success is to understand that networking is an exchange of ideas and information. Be generous and willing to share your talents and experiences and be respectful of contributions from others.

Networking is a thoughtful, well-planned opportunity of introducing yourself to others for the sole purpose of developing your business and material interests. You must do it consistently to get results. **Good networking is about giving**, not the getting, and it takes time to bond with another person. On the other hand, don't appear too enthusiastic. Wait until you have established a reason to give someone your business card.

People will do business with people they respect and trust. Build relationships before you need them. In other words, if you need assistance now, you may need to rely on yesterday's relationships. All that you need to be a successful networker is good communication skills. Remember, most people will be just as nervous as you are, and will respond favorably to someone who is genuinely interested in the success of others.

It's quality over quantity. A network of a hundred names may not be as valuable as ten or twenty solid contacts. Maintain a workable list and manage it like a master networker.

Genuinely,

Bart Smith

TimeToNetwork.com
BartSmith.com
RichCoachBrokeCoach.com
CoachingClientForms.com
SpeakerCafe.com
TVGuest.com
BartsCookies.com
... and many more!

MY NETWORKING BOOKS

If you liked **MY NETWORKING TACTICS,** then you'll definitely want to read my other networking books, which can be found at: **BartSmith.com/books.**

If you love networking as much as I do or maybe you're not the outgoing type and find networking a tad challenging or stressful, well, not to worry.

SIMPLY read this little primer cover to cover highlighting the top **THREE NETWORKING TACTICS** and put into practice every little strategy so your networking efforts will immediately yield maximum results for you and everyone you come in contact with!

INSIDE YOU'LL LEARN:

- Why networking must become a MARKETING PRIORITY for you!

- It's not what you SAY, it's what you ASK! Here's why, how and more!

- Why FOLLOW UP is critical to your networking success and how I do it!

NO ONE IS EXEMPT from making mistakes when they network. EVEN I MAKE MISTAKES! That's why I wrote this book with a good friend of mine. We saw so many people struggling and hosts making unavoidable mistakes.

For example, can you relate? "Did I say the right thing?", "Whoops, that didn't come out right ...", or "Oh, I forgot to bring/do/say this ..." That's our point, and that's why we wrote this book.

Inside *51+ NETWORKING MISTAKES*, we go into REGRETABLE NETWORKING MISTAKES YOU CAN AVOID!

PART I: **BEFORE** NETWORKING
PART II: **WHILE** YOU ARE NETWORKING
PART III: **AFTER** NETWORKING

The cover of the book implies that there are 51+ networking mistakes, but there are so many more! Imagine how much more productive, sharper, your networking experience will be when you know what some of the networking mistakes are ahead of time! Be prepared to get the most quality out of your conversations and your connections!

For MORE INFORMATION and to get this BOOK and/or the AUDIO VERSION, go to:

BartSmith.com/books

BART'S OTHER BOOKS

If you liked **My Networking Tactics**, then you'll definitely want to go to **BartSmith.com** and check out Bart's other books on coaching, personal development, relationships, motivation and more!

SEE MORE BOOKS, EBOOKS & AUDIO AT:

BartSmith.com

ABOUT THE AUTHOR

Bart Smith

TheMarketingMan.com

My Networking Tactics' author, Bart Smith, shares his personal experiences, formulas, communication philosophies, acute human observation as well as his personal tips, tools, tactics, techniques and tricks (which no one else will ever tell you) in the area of *networking* and *working with others* for your benefit, both personally and financially!

Bart Smith, TheMarketingMan.com is the founder and creator of ***MyTrainingCenter.com***, a one-of-a-kind online learning resource center that offers extensive written, audio and video tutorials for computers, business, marketing, speaking, web design and information product creation. With so much specific training in one place, you're bound to give your business, marketing plans, and income potential the boost it needs, both online and offline.

Bart is also the founder of ***BartSmith.com***, a website devoted to personal growth, personal development and anything else where cutting through personal, even political, social and cultural B.S. are concerned.

One of Bart's "fun businesses" is baking the world's best chocolate chip cookies. He's been doing that since his college days. Check out ***BartsCookies.com*** and ***iLoveBartsCookies.com*** ...